The Writer

The Writer

A Guide to Research, Writing,
and Publishing in Biblical Studies

Nijay K. Gupta

CASCADE *Books* • Eugene, Oregon

THE WRITER
A Guide to Research, Writing, and Publishing in Biblical Studies

Copyright © 2022 Nijay K. Gupta. All rights reserved. Except for brief quotations in critical publications or reviews, no part of this book may be reproduced in any manner without prior written permission from the publisher. Write: Permissions, Wipf and Stock Publishers, 199 W. 8th Ave., Suite 3, Eugene, OR 97401.

Cascade Books
An Imprint of Wipf and Stock Publishers
199 W. 8th Ave., Suite 3
Eugene, OR 97401

www.wipfandstock.com

PAPERBACK ISBN: 978-1-7252-9224-6
HARDCOVER ISBN: 978-1-7252-9225-3
EBOOK ISBN: 978-1-7252-9226-0

Cataloguing-in-Publication data:

Names: Gupta, Nijay K.

Title: The writer : a guide to research, writing, and publishing in biblical studies / Nijay K. Gupta.

Description: Eugene, OR: Cascade Books, 2022 | Includes bibliographical references.

Identifiers: ISBN 978-1-7252-9224-6 (paperback) | ISBN 978-1-7252-9225-3 (hardcover) | ISBN 978-1-7252-9226-0 (ebook)

Subjects: LCSH: Authorship | Academic writing | Scholarly publishing | Research—Methodology | Bible—Study and teaching

Classification: PN146 G878 2022 (print) | PN146 (ebook)

"Lots of very smart people with doctorates cannot write very well. And if you can't organize your expertise in such a form that reviewers, editors, and publishers find compelling, all the hard work that went into the PhD will be for naught in a 'publish or perish' world. No other resource contains the same kind of discipline-specific guidance, soft knowledge, and practical wisdom."

—Patrick Gray, Rhodes College

"Few biblical interpreters have been more prolific authors over the course of the past decade or so than Nijay K. Gupta. In *The Writer*, Gupta explores how he goes about the art and craft of research, writing, and publishing, and helps others to see how they might do similarly. Whether you are an aspiring author or a seasoned scholar, you will benefit from the hard-won wisdom that Gupta shares in this volume."

—Todd D. Still, George W. Truett Theological Seminary

"From the nuts and bolts of identifying a research question to choosing the appropriate venue for your work to tailoring your writing for multiple audiences at once, this book is filled with insights to help readers improve their writing while developing their own unique workflow. As one who has published widely and across multiple platforms, Gupta is an expert guide on this journey. Readers will surely benefit from this book!"

—Christopher W. Skinner, Loyola University Chicago

"*The Writer* is a practical guide for students and scholars at any stage in their careers. Gupta helps take the mystery out of the academic writing process, while reminding writers of its gifts and demands. If you wish to learn and teach the nuts and bolts of the research, note-taking, and writing process, this book is for you. It will answer questions you never knew you could ask and will leave you feeling empowered and equipped to get writing."

—Janette H. Ok, Fuller Theological Seminary

"Generously sharing insights honed over years of advising students, Nijay Gupta provides a thorough coverage of the process of researching, writing, and publishing in biblical studies. It's like having your own personal advisor in paper form. I would highly commend this book to anyone considering pursuing research and writing in the field of biblical studies."

—Sydney Elise Tooth, Oak Hill College

"Doing and publishing research in biblical studies can be tricky to navigate. It often feels like entering a new and unknown place. In *The Writer*, Gupta lays out clear steps and provides practical guides to conducting research specifically in biblical studies. This book is like a GPS for anyone who wants to embark on a research journey. Students and aspiring biblical scholars will find it useful and applicable."

—Ekaputra Tupamahu, Portland Seminary

Contents

Preface and Acknowledgments vii

Introduction 1
  Why Write? 1
  My Journey 4

1 Approaching the Problem or Need 9
  Choosing a Topic, Testing Viability 9
  The Deep Dive 10
  Read Outside the Box 11
  NPO and Topic Viability 11
  Exploratory Research 13
  Crowdsource It 13
  Audience 14
  Impact 15
  Writing Form 16
  How Do You Choose a Writing Form? 19

2 A Comprehensive Research and Writing Process 20
  Thinking about a Research Process 21
  Thinking about Method 22
  Step 1: Study (Primary Texts) 23
  Step 2: Discover 25
  Step 3: Study (Secondary) 28
  Step 4: Analyze (Notes) 29
  Step 5: Outline (Draft) 30
  Step 6: Fill (Draft) 31
  Step 7: Version 1 (Draft) 32
  Step 8: Version 2 (Complete) 35
  Step 9: Version 3 (Finalize) 35
  Step 10: Engage (Feedback) 36
  Step 11: Version 4 (Refine) 37
  Pacing the Steps 37
  Final Thoughts 38

Contents

3 The Nuts and Bolts of Research, Note-Taking, and Writing 39
   Building Your Initial Bibliography 39
   Blitzkrieg Research (Step 2) 41
   Taking Notes (Steps 3 and 4) 47

4 Best Practices for Manuscript Writing 53
   Time to Write: Where to Begin? 53
   Overcoming Writer's Block 54
   Finding Your Writing Voice 54
   Use of "I/Me" (Personal Language and Self-Reference in Scholarship) 56
   Sharpening "The Hook": Writing a Good Introduction 57
   "Risk-Writing" 58
   Engaging with Other Scholars 59
   Frequent Summaries 62
   Plagiarism: What Is It, and How to Avoid It 63
   No Writer Is an Island: Create a Feedback System 65
   From Writing to Publication 66

5 Getting Your Work Published 68
   How Do You Make Contact With a Publisher? 70
   The Book Pitch 71
   Writing Up a Book Proposal 72
   Contracts and Expectations 75
   Canceling a Contract? 77
   Do I Need A Literary Agent? 78
   Publishing with Magazines 78

6 Editing and Final Publication Processes 81

7 After the Book Is Published 88
   Reviews of Your Book: The Good, the Bad, and the Ugly 91
   New Editions? 93
   Shaping a Writing Career 93
   Balancing Multiple Projects at Once 95

Appendix A: A Narrative Personal Bibliography 97

Appendix B: Writing and Publishing Advice from Editors in Biblical Studies 111
   Making a Good Book Pitch 111
   Editor Pet Peeves 112
   Becoming Better Writers 113
   Thinking about "Success" 114

Bibliography 115

Preface and Acknowledgments

I THINK OF THIS book as a kind of sequel to *Prepare, Succeed, Advance* (*PSA*). While *PSA* was focused primarily on helping students journey to and through a doctoral program, *The Writer* is concentrated on the art and craft of research, writing, and publishing with a view towards the writing career that comes after completing a doctoral degree. There is some research and writing advice in *PSA*, and a little bit about publication (especially turning the dissertation into a monograph). Also, if you are more interested in publishing academic articles, I would encourage you to look at the relevant sections of *PSA*. *The Writer* offers insights I have gleaned from about fifteen years of professional writing and book publishing.

There are many thanks for me to pass on. I want to acknowledge two editors who have been important collaborators in publishing: Michael Thomson and Chris Spinks. When I was writing this book, I was reminded repeatedly how much both these professionals have shaped my understanding of excellence in publishing. I also want to thank my two doctoral supervisors, Professor John Barclay and Dr. Stephen Barton, for never settling for lazy or mediocre research and writing in my work and for modeling incisive scholarship. When it comes to colleagues who have taught me how to navigate the publishing world, my appreciation goes out to Scot McKnight, Mike Bird, Todd Still, Mike Gorman, Shirley Decker-Lucke, Bryan Dyer, Katya Covrett, Anna Gissing, James Ernest, and Jonathan Pennington. Thanks to some "test readers" of the manuscript: Leo Diaz, Amber Dillon, Jennifer Guo, Dr. Sydney Tooth, and Carrie Wood. Your comments have helped improve this book immensely. Special thanks to my Northern Seminary research assistant Cody Matchett for his meticulous work copyediting and proofreading this book, and making numerous helpful suggestions.

Introduction

You can get a bachelor's degree, master's degree, and a doctorate—and still not really know how to research and write. Degrees often help you know the content and scholarship of your field, but where do you learn *how* to research and write? If you had actual courses on best practices in advanced note-taking and persuasive academic writing, you were one of the lucky ones. In my theological education, I had minimal direct training in any of this. What actually helped me out more than anything else was two journalism courses I had in college. I took those courses as part of a public relations major without any idea that I would end up being a professional writer.

Some people find the craft of writing more natural, others do not. Either way, colleges and seminaries do far too little to prepare "writers" to write. So, students understandably look for guidance elsewhere. There are many good books on the market. I recently enjoyed reading Andy LePeau's succinct and insightful book, *Write Better* (2019), and I would also recommend Helen Sword's books *Stylish Academic Writing* (2012) and *Air and Light and Time and Space: How Successful Academics Write* (2017). Writing in the world of biblical studies is its own special category. This field has its peculiarities and differs significantly from writing a good sermon manuscript or theology blog post.

Why Write?

Before we get too far into the weeds of the best techniques and tools for research and writing, it is crucial that writers spend time discerning why they write at all. Not everyone writes for the same reasons, but it helps to understand what motivates you and what will really satisfy that desire to publish an article, essay, or book. Let me say, while I affirm there are many reasons for writing, and each person has to discover their own niche and calling as a writer, I do think there are some bad reasons for writing and publishing. For example, if you think it is a pathway to making lots of money, *think again*. To make major income on book royalties requires a number of things falling into place at once: incredible ideas, ability to be marketed to large reading populations, a smooth and attractive writing style (harder to achieve than most readers and writers think), a publisher devoted to your work, and a major public platform (which normally involves many thousands of social media followers). The vast majority of published writers in biblical studies do not make much "return on investment" money from their books.[1] Publishing is seen as a contribution to scholarship, a hobby, and/or a ministry.

From a Christian perspective, I think the most sustaining motivation for writing, and one that will have the best chance of leading to a satisfying experience beginning to end, is treating it as a gift and a calling. Some people, I fear, just assume that writing a book will make them famous. Or it is, perhaps, a box to tick on a bucket list (*I've always wanted to write a book!*). But writing is hard work for most people—harder than new writers often imagine, and the process is long and involves many people, parts, and stages. So, there needs to be a deeper passion that drives the work.

To see writing as a "gift" means that you feel that you have been *given* something to say. It might be a new idea. It may be a fresh perspective on current events in the world or in your community. It could be a pivotal correction to the field of study. Perhaps it is a popularization of an esoteric concept. Maybe it is applying a well-known idea to another context. Whatever it is, you feel that you were given insight and a writing voice to speak out.

That "gift" often develops into a conviction and a calling. For writing to be a gift and calling means that the writer has to devote time and energy to the work, specifically to doing it right and ensuring it actually does make an impact on the target audience. That means that other things in life will get less time; sometimes the writer has to lessen their "day-job" workload

---

1. Just for "fun," one time I calculated how many hours I worked on a book and then how much money in royalties I made over about three years after its release. My per-hour pay came out to around $.50! Obviously I couldn't make a reasonable income off of that rate, but I loved every minute of researching and writing that book, so it's not about the money for me, it's about the personal and professional satisfaction. Most academics see royalties as a "perk" of writing, and not income they can count on to pay the bills.

or release certain other commitments. A distracted writer trying to juggle work, family, and hobbies often doesn't produce great, timely work. That should be obvious, but the reality for many academics is that writing tends to be a small part of one's life, not the main occupation. Thus, it is all too easy for writing to be the extra thing on the pile of life commitments that gets neglected or perpetually delayed.

Of course, becoming a good writer does not mean you have to neglect your family, cut off your friends, stop playing tennis, or quit your job. But I do want to underscore from the outset the foundational importance of "counting the cost." If you treat writing a book as an ethereal aspiration, you will either never finish the work, create an insubstantial contribution, or fail to impact your audience. As you ponder whether you really want to do the work of a writer, make sure you consider these questions.

Education: Do I already have the background and knowledge required to make an accurate and meaningful contribution to the subject that I want to write on? Do I need to take more courses or get a(nother) degree? Am I equipped to be an expert on the things that I am writing about?

Time: Do I have time over a long period, on a regular basis, to devote to research, writing, and production (manuscript revising, indexing, reading page proofs, marketing, etc.)?

Passion: Do I love the subject enough to spend hundreds of hours in research, writing, and promotion of the book?

There is one more consideration that I did not fully understand before I started my writing career: dealing with negative criticism and bad reviews. This has been the worst part of my experience as a writer. To be a writer *is* to be criticized. That's a fact I didn't understand until reading reviews of my work in journals and on blogs and websites. Will some people love your work? Probably. (*My mom always says nice things!*) But inevitably there will be negative words written or spoken about you and your work. It comes with the territory. Sure, some negative reviews are inaccurate and some are just plain mean. But whatever the case, no author is immune from criticism and the most decorated writers get negative reviews. So, you have to be prepared for that as well. Actually, you can't *really* prepare yourself for bad reviews except to do the best research and writing you can (and get solid feedback in the process from colleagues and your editor) and just *know* ahead of time some people will not like your work and will share their thoughts with others. We will discuss how to handle negative reviews later (chapter 7), but for now I simply want to acknowledge that writing puts you and your work in the public sphere—some readers may want to hoist you up on their shoulders and parade you around giving glowing commendations for your ideas. But others will throw virtual rotten tomatoes and digital stinky eggs at you. Either way, if you are a person that "just wants to be left alone"—well, don't publish.

My Journey

Before we get much further in this book, I thought I would share a bit of my journey into research and writing. This might help you understand where I am coming from and how my life has shaped my body of work. (A more detailed personal bibliography narrative appears in Appendix A.)

Let's start with college. I wasn't a great writer in those days. I wasn't even a good writer. I admit that I didn't invest much time in writing quality papers. I did passable work. In seminary, I had more of a passion for the subjects I was studying, and, to be honest, I cared more about impressing my professors. So, I put more thought and energy into writing research papers, but, alas, my writing was still not very good. What was the problem? First, I didn't have a *plan* for tackling the papers—I just "wrote" them. Also, looking back I can probably say that I wasn't an invested and devoted *reader*, and we all know the best writers are avid readers. You tend to emulate the quality and, to some degree, style of the books you read. I definitely increased my reading in seminary, but my writing ability only improved a little bit.

One thing that really helped me in seminary was learning how to do exegesis (methodical interpretation) of biblical texts, especially analyzing the literary structure of a passage. This is beneficial for studying biblical texts, but it is also helpful for studying *any* text past or present.[2]

During my doctoral studies, I continued to strengthen my research and writing skills, especially as I intentionally examined each aspect of my process, from conception to completion. One of the big "needs" I had at this time was learning how to take notes well, figuring out where to store them and how to organize them, and then how best to use them in my work.

---

2. On biblical exegesis, read Gorman, *Elements of Biblical Exegesis*; I also commend the classic, Adler and Van Doren, *How to Read a Book*.

Introduction

Since the completion of my PhD (now more than a decade ago!), I have had lots of trial-and-error experiences in research, writing, and publishing. I have written twelve books (and edited a handful more), I have published about two dozen articles, and I have blogged regularly since 2007. For six years, I led the research program at Portland Seminary and taught advanced research and writing every year. Writing has become a significant part of my life. Some people write occasionally, but I consider myself a "writer." On average, I spend about half of my work week doing research or writing.

If I could go back and say a few things to my 2006 (first-year PhD student) self, I would offer three things:

1. Take meticulous notes on everything relevant to your research, especially books you loaned (e.g., interlibrary loan) that you don't own. Save those notes, you might use the material for a later project, even if it doesn't seem "relevant" now.

2. Be brave! Don't just toe the line of consensus scholarship. Push beyond the boundaries to argue new things of importance. Writing isn't about receiving a "medal of participation" for publishing a book. It is about making a bona fide contribution to knowledge.

3. Find your writing voice. Don't just sum up scholarship or weave together quotes from other writers. Yes, engage with academic scholarship and acknowledge when you are depending on the ideas of one person or another, but your book should be *your book*. Your work should have *your* voice.

This is just a taste of the journey I have been on for the past decade and a half. My "authoring" path was very windy with lots of bumps, a few sudden stops, and the occasional wrong turns. Thus, I thought I would attempt to pass on some of my lessons learned to others who want to avoid some of the pitfalls I experienced. Here is a snapshot of what you can expect in the chapters of this book. I recognize that different kinds of readers will be interested in different sections of this book, so there is no shame in skipping around and reading selections that seem more interesting or useful to you! You can refer back to the Table of Contents page for a closer look at the subheadings and specific matters addressed in each chapter.

Approaching the Problem or Need. First, we begin at the place where all book ideas start—a problem or "gap" in knowledge. Usually a book idea doesn't come "all at once," but forms over time as you feel uneasy or unhappy with what literature has been published in a particular area. We will explore how to identify and clarify that problem or need. Until you have sufficiently explored the problem, you can't really address a "solution." Here we will also consider the "audience" of the book. One of the biggest mistakes that writers make is having a fuzzy impression of the intended book audience, or trying to communicate to too many different audiences at once. Trying to write to multiple audiences is like "blended worship"—it may *feel* like a win-win, but in the end everyone feels unsatisfied.

A Comprehensive Research and Writing Process. This chapter is more theoretical than the subsequent ones. It looks at the big picture of shaping the writing project and communicating ideas effectively. We will talk about methods, "conversation partners," determining the "big ideas" of the book, persuasive forms of argumentation and evidence, finding the right writing "tone," and reflecting on bias and personal blindspots.

The Nuts and Bolts of Research, Note-Taking, and Writing. Something that I have worked *a lot* on in the last ten years has been fine-tuning the way I collect and organize my notes. I cannot overestimate how crucial this is for making the writing process smooth and efficient. Taking the time and effort to have a well-thought-through system will save you many hours. Here I will offer personal tips and walk you through my own systems.

Best Practices for Manuscript Writing. This is the chapter where I give advice about the writing of the book manuscript. Writing is not just stitching together notes. It is certainly not just putting pen to paper or clicking keys on your keyboard. All writers seek to find their "voice." All writers struggle with writers' block. All writers have anxieties and doubts about their own work. We will consider these matters and offer some counsel for developing a writer's mindset and habits that are healthy and sustainable.

Getting Your Work Published. The successful writer is not done when the manuscript is written. "Authoring" is a team sport and the publisher plays an important role in the whole process. More and more I am recognizing how instrumental it is to find the right publisher for your work. I will offer advice on choosing a publisher, writing a strong proposal (with supporting materials), and creating a healthy relationship with your editorial and production team.

Introduction

We will also look at different forms of publication beyond just books. Perhaps your ideas and writing style might work better for a different genre such as a magazine or blog. Books, of course, will always be around, but now there are so many other options for publications and it is worth asking the type/platform questions.

Editing and Final Publication Processes. Once a writer finishes a manuscript and sends it to the publisher, an important checkpoint has been reached, but the work is far from over. There is a back-and-forth revision process that most publishers have with the goal of refining and transforming the work into a finished product, i.e., a good book. Writers work closely with their editor, perhaps a separate copyeditor, and then also possibly engage with aspects of the book like back cover copy, cover design, and endorsements. Somewhere in this process, the author is usually expected to produce the book indexes—not a favorite activity for anyone, but a necessary task in the process.

After the Book Is Published. The author's work is not even done after the editing process! Before I had ever published a book, I assumed that the process was this: (1) identify a good book idea, (2) research the book, (3) write the book, (4) publish the book, (5) go out and celebrate, (6) move on. Steps 1–4 are true and important, and I definitely recommend that you take time to celebrate 5, but if you "move on" to the next project too quickly, you are missing out on opportunities to engage your audience *after* the book is out. Since you have put so much blood, sweat, and tears (yes, sometimes there are tears!) into this labor of love, you will want to support the book's "life" in the world. We will discuss what it takes to get the book on the radar and into the hands of as many as possible in your target audience. This is an oft-neglected, sometimes awkward, life-stage of the book, but it is important to achieving the goals of writing—that the work actually influences readers and makes a contribution to knowledge.

In chapter 1, we will begin where all good books start: a need.

1

Approaching the Problem or Need

A GOOD WRITING PROJECT often begins in the same place: with a feeling or an inkling that something is *not right* or something is *missing* in an area of study. When I worked at Portland Seminary advising doctor of ministry students, my colleagues and DMin program directors Dr. Loren Kerns and Dr. Clifford Berger always encouraged students to start their project with an "NPO" concept and statement—Need/Problem/Opportunity. Projects that don't start with an NPO can easily end up just being topical "chatter." Without an NPO, such writing attempts can lack urgency and fail to make an impact. I remember one of my doctoral program professors confessing that he hates research projects that are subtitled "Explorations in . . . " or "Exploring . . . " *How can you present a thesis answer to a research question when all you are doing is "exploring"?* Fair point. Thesis-driven writing must start with a real problem or need. The problem could be that a topic has not been addressed, or that something has been misunderstood. Or that certain approaches and tools could shed new light on a certain problem. Whatever the exact case, a "problem/need" is necessary before an "answer/solution" is given.

Choosing a Topic, Testing Viability

Students often ask me: How do you choose a topic to begin with? When I was exploring doctoral programs, I remember emailing a few potential doctoral advisors and asking something like: *What topics do you suggest for new research?* This seemed like a reasonable question to me because *they* are the experts. Surely they know where the research "gaps" exist, where the needs, problems, and opportunities are. Sometimes they would send me some ideas, sometimes not, but this piece of advice was often included: *students should come up with their own research topics, because it should derive from their own passions and interests.* For a doctoral dissertation, for example, the research and writing takes three to five years, at least, and for this to sustain the student's attention, it must develop out of something they are really interested in. It is basically the same for all book ideas—there is something nagging you in the pit of your stomach, or pestering you like a splinter in your mind, and you just have to research and write to resolve or address it. So, topic and NPO need to come out of our own passions, interests, and life experiences. Sure, you can ask experts to test and refine your thoughts, but it should start with *your* interests.

Let's say you understand all of this, but you still don't know what to research and write about (for a master's thesis, for example). What do you do? How do you know enough about a subject to know what the problems are? Where do the "gaps" exist?

The Deep Dive

Here's one idea: Read a lot of literature in one area of study, a literature binge, if you will.[3] You will start to get a grasp of the currents and conventional views in your field. Read book reviews, read journal articles, and notice where "pressure points" lie. My experience has been, once you get into the weeds of a sub-discipline, and you have a strong grasp of what has been written and where there are established views on major issues, you start to see where there is room and need for something else to say. Keep in mind, the goal is not to find something "brand new." Very few books say something no one has *ever* said before. Usually, nonfiction contributions refine, nuance, correct, and enhance. Often, they bring a new conversation partner to the table of discussion, which may come in the form of new tools and methods, or bringing texts or worlds into conversation in a fresh way.

---

3. If you are a master's student, or even in a bachelor's program, you could propose this as an independent study where you dig deep in reading into a specific topic of interest. I did this in seminary as an independent study and I have supervised such studies as a professor.

Here's a tip: Read long, academic reviews of the key works in your field. Really good critical book reviews are able to point out blindspots in influential literature. That can stimulate ideas and point you in some helpful directions for shedding new light on a subject.

Read Outside the Box

This advice is kind of the opposite of the one above. Instead of the narrow deep dive, you might find inspiration by looking *outside* your discipline. When ten thousand people have already studied your subject for centuries, it is truly hard to find something "new" to talk about. But I have found that a fresh perspective can often be achieved by spending time in another discipline. Sometimes a methodology or insight from outside can be brought in to bring a new angle to the conversation. For example, insights from social science, psychology, or cultural anthropology.

NPO and Topic Viability

Okay, let's say you have an NPO in mind. How do you know if it is viable? How do you know if it is worth pursuing, worth researching, worth publishing? It is helpful to keep in mind that academic research is all about *experimentation*. There is no way to know at the beginning of a new research project whether it will pan out. Research is a discovery process. Sometimes it works out, sometimes it doesn't. Sometimes you strike gold with an idea and you discover that you had something really important to say that has been neglected before. Other times, you get excited about an idea, only to discover eventually that someone already beat you to it. Or the material just doesn't go anywhere. So, all that to say, you can't know at the very beginning whether it will "work out." It is very possible your time will be wasted on research. But, in fact, that's the nature of the game. It's like going fishing (so fishermen tell me); you do the same tedious preparation and sometimes you don't catch any fish that day, or that week, or that month. (If it's been a year, find another fishing spot and question your life choices.) But sometimes you catch *more* than you expected. That's a good day, enjoy it.

Having made all of these provisos, I do think we can say a few things about this that might put you at ease in that early stage of NPO crafting and hypothesis development. There is a balance of existing academic scholarship that you want to look for. It is a game of threading the needle and there may be signs (on one side or the other) that the idea is just not going to work out.

Not Enough Scholarship. So, let's say you have an idea for research, and you go to the academic databases to see what is already out there on your subject. Let's say there is *nothing* at all (or *almost* nothing). In one sense that might be good, fresh territory to explore. But in another sense, that might be a red flag. Is it possible (almost) *no one* has written on this in modern history? Maybe that's for a reason. In that case, maybe there is just no traction. What progress can you gain without dialogue partners?[4] Sometimes, the topic is just too speculative, and there is not enough material to do solid academic exploration.

Too Much Scholarship. Or, what if you have the opposite problem? You have what *you* think is a great topic. You are fired up and ready to say something—only to discover, lots of people have been talking about this for a long time and have said *basically* what you want to say. That doesn't mean it is a complete wash. Sometimes you can dig a bit deeper and see "what else" needs to be said. But, to be honest, in many cases it is wise to throw in the towel and admit that it is not workable. Let me give an example from my own experience. A few years back, I had a great idea. I wanted to write a book on Paul's theology of the mind and how the gospel transforms the way we think. I started to sketch out research questions, I began to assemble key Pauline passages, I did initial soundings in Pauline scholarship; yes, I found a few treatments here and there, but not really a substantial book-length work. So, *voila!*, there was "room" for a contribution. Aha! *Except*, not long after I crafted this brilliant book idea (I even had a publisher in mind), I saw a forthcoming book announcement from my friend Craig Keener, *The Mind of the Spirit*. And, just like that, my book idea was dead. Sure, I could have written *another* book on the subject, but as I got a chance to look at Keener's book, it covered pretty much what I wanted to say. I emailed Craig both to congratulate him *and* to give him a hard time: "Craig, you stole my book idea!" Without missing a beat, he responded, "You should thank me, because now you don't have to write it!" (Cue "Debbie Downer" sound effect.)

---

4. Later on (chapter 3) we will be talking about the initial stages of building your bibliography and making sure you "find" as much relevant material as you can. There may be more out there, and the question is how to find it. But sometimes there really is not very much.

Approaching the Problem or Need

Back to viability: keep in mind, rarely does the initial research question and initial thesis idea stay with the project through to the very end in the precise original form. It is a starting place, but often both question and hypothesis get tweaked and refined and adjusted as the research is conducted. That's natural and healthy. In fact, rigidly trying to prove your original thesis without being open to "where the research leads" is bad form. The thesis idea must be held with an open hand—*this is what I think is going on, but I will adjust as I get into the details of scholarship and learn more about the subject.*

So, how do you test the viability of your research question and basic hypothesis?

Exploratory Research

Start with quick and rough "exploratory research" (not Google). Get into some academic research databases (more on that in chapter 3) and perform an initial search on keywords that will call up studies in your field. If you see right away that your subject has been adequately covered, in particular that your research question has been addressed sufficiently, then you know you are going to be entering a crowded field. But if you discover that you cannot find much on your topic that has already been published, that might be a clue that a "gap" exists that you can fill. That doesn't mean things won't change as you discover more relevant literature, but it does give you a bit of confidence that you can move forward in your research.

Crowdsource It

To be honest, it helps to reach out to colleagues and friends and ask if your topic and NPO are fresh. You want to make sure you are asking the right people, people in your field with knowledge of the subject. The reality is, sometimes we live too much in our own headspace and it helps to get another set of eyes on the subject. Invite others to give you honest feedback on your ideas.[5]

---

5. This reminds me of the Seinfeld-ism—*is this something?* Comedian Jerry Seinfeld explains how part of his creative process when trying out new jokes involves doing check-ins with peers. *Is this something?*, as in, *is this actually funny to you?* Similarly, we might ask our colleagues: *is this a legitimate problem? Do you see the same "gap/need" that I do?*

Audience

One of the first things you need to get straight in your mind when planning to write is: *Who is my audience? Who am I trying to persuade?* You might think—*everyone!* But the reality is, aim for *everyone* and you end up reaching *no one.* You need to try and actually imagine, *who would buy my book? Who would search for this in a library catalog? Who would click on this as a suggested product on a shopping website? If I put on a conference on the subject of my book, who would come, and who would sit in the front row on the edge of their seat?*

Discovering and discerning your writing audience has to do with shared affinity and expertise. Who else has some interest and expertise in what you are writing about? Perhaps there is an element of education involved. Does your writing use technical language that expects specialist knowledge (like Koine Greek, ancient history, or biblical literacy)? Or is the audience a certain occupation group (like pastors, chaplains, or teachers)? Alternatively, you may be wanting to reach an audience that knows very little about the subject, and you want to pique their curiosity. It's important that you get that right in your early considerations.

One way to get a sense for your audience is to look at similar books and literature. Look at comments on social media: who is interested in those other similar books? Look at Amazon and GoodReads reviews: what kind of people are reviewing it? Look at the back cover endorsers: what does that tell you about the audience? Would you want the same kinds of endorsers to promote *your* book? That will give you some clues as to your audience.

Now, I already said it makes no sense to cast your net too wide when it comes to audience. You want to find "your people," whoever they are, and figure out how to get them interested in what you have to say. But you also don't want to think too narrowly. I like to think in terms of concentric circles. The "bullseye" is your target audience, the primary folks you have in mind as you write. But one more circle out could be people who have *some* interest in what you have to say. You don't want to cater to that audience, but it is wise to keep them in mind. For example, I wrote a somewhat technical book called *Paul and the Language of Faith*. In terms of readership, I had in mind academics like myself and seminary students, but I also knew that pastors would be interested in a book like this on Pauline theology, so when I wrote the book I said in the introduction that readers who weren't wanting to wade through some of the Greek-heavy early sections could skip to later chapters. I made sure that, throughout the book, I put in good chapter introductions and end-summaries, knowing pastors might need to skim parts of it, because they were just looking for the "big ideas" and the "so whats." I also made my final chapter pretty robust, with an extended mapping out of what I learned in the big picture about Paul's conception of faith. Now, of course I wanted readers to read the whole book, beginning to end; my assumption was that my primary audience (the "bullseye") would do that. But I also knew there were some things I could do pretty easily in the book to make it useful to a secondary audience ("next circle out") without losing sight of my primaries. Another example: for my book *Reading Philippians*, the main audience was seminary students and pastors who wanted a lower-level academic introduction to this Pauline text. But I also thought that it *could* serve as a kind of academic "Bible study" for personal edification or a group study at church. So, I made sure some of the end-of-chapter discussion questions were geared towards formation and spiritual growth. Part of what I am saying is that it doesn't take much, if you plan ahead, to make your work accessible and useful to a secondary audience. But it is important to draw those audience circles early and clearly to streamline your research and writing agenda.

Again, everything can and should be tweaked and refined as you go. Nothing is set in stone in early stages of conception and research. You can change your mind. But I have found that having a sense of audience, even at the outset, gives some clarity to the wider objective of the writing project.

One thing to consider: have two or three *real* people you know in mind as you think about the book. Maybe even put their names at the top of your research document. This might help you stay focused and clear. One of the dangers that I warn my students about in their writing: sometimes writers write to assuage or please *reviewers* rather than the target audience. That can sometimes endanger the success of the book. Your editors are (ideally) trained to help make sure your work is accurate and avoid drawing unfair criticism from reviewer; your job as a writer is to hit the bullseye with your target reader.

Impact

It is also beneficial to consider what level of impact you want to have on your target audience. You can't honestly expect your written works to always transform the life of the reader. I am currently in the process of editing a large dictionary. Very few are going to pick up this dictionary and walk away with new purpose in life. Most of the dictionary articles are short and meant to give students a quick understanding of a topic. For nonfiction, we can break down impact into roughly three categories:

Basic information. Textbooks and introductory kinds of resources often have the goal of offering overview-like information. They help students to orient themselves to the subject matter.

Advanced information. Many academic resources, books and articles, expect that their readers already have some grasp of the subject. They are working with a more narrow, specialized, trained audience who want to take their knowledge to a deeper level.

Thesis-driven. Some works are "thesis-driven" in the sense that the writer is arguing in favor of a particular set of original ideas with the intention of influencing the reader to accept these ideas. Textbooks, for example, are not typically thesis-driven; they tend to be "neutral" and desire to capture the "state of the discipline." Academic articles in peer-reviewed periodicals tend to be thesis-driven because they publish persuasive, original research.

When writing offers *basic information*, the intent for impact is *knowledge*. The writer seeks to inform. When it comes to *advanced information*, the intent is *mastery*. With *thesis-driven* research, the intent is *influence* towards a way of looking at a subject. Now, sometimes the lines between these things are not neat, but this is a helpful starting point to think about what you really want out of your work.

Writing Form

There are many ways to get your ideas out there into the world. There are academic articles, magazine articles, books, blogs, podcasts. It's worth thinking through the best writing form.

Academic Monograph. For academics, the expectation of a doctoral dissertation is that it will be published as an academic monograph. A monograph is typically defined as a detailed and technical single-author work driven by a thesis. From the publisher's end, such books are vetted carefully for academic excellence, sometimes even contacting the doctoral examiners. Because the audience for monographs is limited, they are not priced for

Approaching the Problem or Need

individual purchase. Monograph publishers often print a small number of books and focus on getting the volumes into academic libraries. In biblical studies, there are numerous monograph series that collect volumes that share similar topics, approaches, or focus on one ancient corpus or era of history.

Basic Textbook. A basic textbook in biblical studies is aimed at the beginner student in college or graduate school. These tend to be relatively short, easy to read, and do not presume previous technical knowledge of the reader. Publishers are careful about who writes basic textbooks. They want to ensure textbooks have a wide audience, so it helps for the author to have a strong reputation in their field. It is not impossible for early career scholars to write basic textbooks, but in those cases a good book spreads through word of mouth from students and professors and becomes a kind of "sleeper" success.

Advanced Textbook. Advanced textbooks are meant to take students to the next level of their understanding of a subject. The audience tends to be upper-level college students and graduate students. They have a smaller audience than basic textbooks because they require some technical knowledge of readers.

Reference Work. Biblical studies benefits from all manner of reference works, from dictionaries to atlases to handbooks, commentaries, and lexicons. The idea behind a reference work is that it is not read "cover to cover," but used or "referenced" as needed. Think about a Bible dictionary—the student or pastor might pull it off the shelf to look up a person, event, or concept. Occasionally a reference work is written by a single author, but often multiple scholars with their unique specialties come together in a collected work. In biblical studies, an especially popular resource is the Bible commentary. Commentaries have a long history, going back to the patristic era. The typical Bible commentary addresses matters of background and situation for a biblical text, and then "comments" verse-by-verse or section-by-section. Most commentaries employ a blend of methods (literary, socio-historical, rhetorical, theological), some apply a specific lens (womanist, ecological, etc.).

Trade Book. Sometimes it is hard to understand book publishing lingo, especially in biblical studies where there is readership overlap between the academic world and the world of pastors and laypeople. A "trade book" is intended for a general audience, sometimes called "popular level." These are non-technical books that cast the audience net wide. Pastors and Christian social influencers write trade books in the wider Christian community, but sometimes academics write trade books as well. Publishers of trade books are cautious about their authors, carefully selecting voices that will find and impact a wide audience.

Cross-Over Book. This is not industry language as far as I can tell, but something I hear now and again. Some books are "crossover" in the sense that they are written by academics with some technical information but also may find a broader (trade) audience. N. T. Wright, Scot McKnight, Amy-Jill Levine, and James K. A. Smith are all examples of scholars who have found success in trade and "crossover" publication. But it is important to know that these writers are the exception insofar as they have written on the right topics at the right times with the right platform and expertise and a dash of luck to sell thousands and thousands of copies of their books. Their stories are not the normal stories of publishing by academics!

Aside from books, there are other media for publication worth thinking about.

Academic Article. A staple of publication for academics is the article, a relatively short (let's say 6,000- to 10,000-word) engagement with a narrow subject, often thesis-driven like monographs, but on a smaller scale. Academic articles are reviewed carefully by an editorial committee. There are different kinds of journals with different systems, but the academic standard is "blind peer review," which entails a process of assessment where the reviewer(s) do not know the identity of the article author. Some academic institutions expect their faculty to publish academic articles for their professional review.

Magazine Article. There is also the magazine article. Sometimes it is a bit difficult to discern whether a periodical is a journal or a magazine. The general rules of thumb I use to detect the difference involve (1) audience, (2) solicitation, (3) assessment, and (4) payment. Magazines have a much broader, "popular" audience. Think about magazines like *Christian Century*, *Sojourners*, and *Christianity Today*. Secondly, with academic journals, for the most part authors send in articles for review. With magazines, an editor or team of editors solicit articles, sometimes with a theme in mind. Third, when a magazine article is solicited by an editor, there is a process of editing, but it is not usually a "blind" process. Lastly, academic journal articles do not involve payment to the author—at least, I've never been paid! But often magazines offer payment to writers (e.g., per-word payment, or lump sum). There is no clear industry standard for amount; it depends on the income structure of the magazine.

How Do You Choose a Writing Form?

When considering the writing form, you have to take into consideration (a) expertise, (b) audience, (c) impact, (d) platform, (e) time, and (f) passions. *Do you have the expertise and technical knowledge to write a monograph or advanced textbook? Who do you imagine as your audience? How do you want to impact readers? Do you have the platform to write a magazine article or trade book? Do you have time to write a reference work? What do you want to do?* Sometimes the answers to these questions are simple and clear. In other cases, you have to have some conversations with friends, colleagues, mentors, and editors.

In this chapter, we looked at the very beginnings of the process of research and writing. Before you dive into writing or publishing, you need to have some clarity about why you are writing, what topic interests you have, and some initial thoughts about the writing form and media. *Only fools rush in*, they say, and they are right. It pays in the end for writers to patiently invest in the first set of questions about the who, what, why (and maybe also the how). Later on, you can address the where and when. The first step, in my opinion, is really figuring out the NPO (Need, Problem, Opportunity). If this isn't clear, it will be hard to get the research going and the publication off the ground. The NPO may shift a bit or evolve over time—that's a normal and healthy process of discovery, research, and refinement—but that is still the heart of the work of writing. At first, the NPO might be fuzzy, but as you study and read and reflect, you should be able to see and feel more and more of an urgency for that NPO to be addressed. If you have discovered a viable NPO, you are off to a great start.

2

A Comprehensive Research and Writing Process

LET'S SAY YOU HAVE a writing passion, you have identified an NPO and you have a feel for writing form, audience, and impact. That's an exciting feeling, I know it well. There is this rush knowing that potential exists for solving a problem, meeting a need, starting or contributing to an important conversation. So, you sit down at your desk and open up your computer to get started on "research." [. . . . .] NOW WHAT?

It's funny, I tell people who are not academics that I spend a good part of my week, my job, doing "research." But what doess that *actually* mean? What really *is* research? Research is a discovery, study, and analysis process of learning, answering questions, and testing ideas. When you try to figure out which kind of car to buy, and where to buy it, you do research. When you have a weird rash and want to know if it is a "see the doctor" kind of issue, you do research. When you want to watch a particular movie, but don't know if it is worth your time, you do research. It's an information-gathering and sifting activity.

The sad thing is that when it comes to religious studies, it is too often the case that many of us were never taught exactly *how* to do research. There is this impression that you go to the library and "research" magically happens. But I remember feeling alone and uneasy during my doctoral studies. Several teachers handed me *tools* for research (e.g., database links), but no one really showed me how to use the tools and, perhaps more importantly, how all these things work together as one big activity we call "research."

A Comprehensive Research and Writing Process

Having a specific method and approach will hopefully save writers time and energy and give them a more satisfying experience.

Thinking about a Research Process

In this chapter, I will walk through my own research process. Now, this is obviously not the only way to do research. This is just *my* way, and I don't always follow this procedure rigidly. Sometimes I skip steps, sometimes I perform steps simultaneously, etc. If you are relatively new to research, or you don't yet have your own system in place, I suggest that you try this out and see what is most useful to you. Then you can tweak the process to suit your own preferences, personality, context, and needs. It's kind of like following a recipe. You try it, then you try it again and make adjustments to suit your own preferences and taste.

Here is the overview of the steps:

1. **Study (Primary Literature):** Study primary texts for yourself, take notes and postulate theories
2. **Discover:** Discover and acquire secondary (bibliographical) items
3. **Study (Secondary Literature):** Study secondary scholarship, working from general resources to specific
4. **Analyze:** Re-organize, analyze, and synthesize notes
5. **Outline:** Sketch your text outline and flow (include your main points and big ideas)
6. **Fill:** Tie notes to sections
7. **Draft** (Writing stage 1): Write initial draft
8. **Complete** (Writing stage 2): Refine and complete your work
9. **Finalize** (Writing stage 3): Iron out wrinkles and conform to appropriate academic style
10. **Engage:** Solicit feedback from peers
11. **Refine:** (Writing stage 4): Refine again after receiving feedback

The Writer
Thinking about Method

Before we run through this eleven-step process of research, it is important to think from the outset about interpretive methods in biblical studies. Sometimes students don't put much thought into methodology because it is like lenses—something you look *through* so you sometimes don't even *see* them. But good researchers are keenly aware of the methods they are using in research. Now is not the place to give a comprehensive discussion of methods and approaches in biblical research. But allow me here to just talk through some methods to illustrate how different approaches, lenses, and tools can open up different kinds of things in research.[1]

Historical. A historical analysis is focused on events, circumstances, and settings in the past. When we study the Bible, we are engaging in a set of texts written many hundreds of years ago by people in cultures and contexts that most of us are not readily familiar with. A *historian's* toolkit is equipped to examine ancient texts carefully in historical context.

Literary. The Bible is literature, obviously. When we study texts *as* literature, we are thinking about how and why people write things to inform, persuade, entertain, inspire, and provoke. The *literary critic's* toolkit helps us see the artistry and craft that goes into poetry versus story-telling versus incisive rhetoric (etc.)

Social-scientific. The Bible is about people. Or at least people are often the focus of biblical texts. The social sciences offer insight into communities and relationships. The *social scientist's* toolkit draws from disciplines like social anthropology, politics, social psychology, and sociology to help us make sense of patterns of interactive human behavior.

Reception studies. Reception studies recognize that different people, in different places, in different eras of history have engaged with the Bible in different ways. Rather than simply getting to the *one true meaning* of a text, reception scholars are interested in how biblical texts have left an impact on people, communities, and culture throughout history. The *reception scholar's* toolkit helps us to analyze the world *in front of* the text, recognizing that we (today) are not the first or only people to study the Bible.

---

1. Recommended reading on methods and approaches: see Edwards, "Hermeneutics and Exegesis," and Gorman, *Scripture and Its Intepretation*.

A Comprehensive Research and Writing Process

Location readings. Readers bring themselves to the practice of reading any text. I am Asian-American, I read all texts from my own culture, experiences, heritage, and value system. And there are things that I "see" in the text that others don't. We can all benefit from learning from one another's vantage point. The *location-perspective* toolkit helps us see our own blindspots and find value and meaning in the perspectives of others.

I could go on and on and on about a plethora of methods that can be used—many in combination—for research and to stimulate fresh thought. But what I want to emphasize here is that it is crucial to have a long think about methodology early on in the research process. Don't just "wing it." Don't just do what your professor does, or what other students are doing. Take some time to process what approaches, tools, and lenses are going to help you the most in addressing your NPO. Now, having said that, it is not always simple or straightforward to make decisions about method right at the beginning. You might want to sketch out some initial thoughts, and then make a more firm decision after conducting some research and seeing what scholars have done or have missed (steps 1–3).

Step 1: Study (Primary Texts)

It should go without saying—but I'm going to say it anyway—*make sure to spend ample time working with your primary texts.* These are the ancient texts that are the focus of your study. I find that students and writers sometimes appear too eager to jump into the secondary (especially modern) scholarship. The effect of this is that they end up *relying* on other scholars rather than trying to glean their own insights from direct and extensive engagement with the primary texts.

So, if you are writing on Philemon, make sure you are actually spending time studying the text of Philemon itself, not just scholarship *about* Philemon. If you can study it in Greek, all the better. But the same advice goes for ancient texts related to your main text(s). So, sticking with the Philemon scenario, I am disappointed to find that scholars tend to read and repeat dictionary information about ancient slavery rather than reading primary texts about ancient slavery (from inscriptions, personal letters, ancient fiction portraying the lives of slaves, etc.). Here is a point I want to reiterate throughout this book: *don't blindly trust secondary sources!* Always have this question in the back of your mind as you engage with secondary scholarship—*have they supplied specific evidence to back up their claims or support their views?* Often it is the case that direct and clear evidence is not given. Sometimes the claim is true anyway, but I find that sometimes it is misleading, inaccurate, or just plain wrong. So . . . read the primary texts for yourself. No reader expects the writer to have read *every possible relevant primary text*, but have a research mentality of looking things up for yourself and doing your own fact-checking.

A natural question to ask at this stage is—how do you actually find the primary texts? If you are working with the Bible, in Hebrew the standard is BHS, in Greek the NA28 and UBS5 (keep an eye out for new updated versions). If you are in search of the ancient texts written around the time of biblical literature, I suggest checking out two handy books: Kenton Sparks, *Ancient Texts for the Study of the Hebrew Bible*, and Craig A. Evans, *Ancient Texts for New Testament Studies*. These books do not contain primary texts in full, but explain where to find original language versions and English translations of them. Perhaps you won't find everything you need in Sparks and Evans, but you will be off to a good start with the most important parallel texts.

Another key resource is the Loeb Classical Library. This set provides Greek and Latin texts and English translations of the most important works from the Classical era. In biblical studies and Classics these are considered respected translations that can be used in scholarship. For early Jewish literature, check out: Susan Docherty, *The Jewish Pseudepigrapha: An Introduction to the Literature of the Second Temple Period*, Daniel M. Gurtner, *Introducing the Pseudepigrapha of Second Temple Judaism*, and George Nickelsburg, *Jewish Literature between the Bible and the Mishnah: Second Edition*.

It is crucially important to sit down with these primary texts and jot down your own thoughts, insights, reflections, and notes at an early stage. Later on, when you have spent hours upon hours looking at secondary scholarship, it will be hard to separate your "fresh thought" on the primary texts from what you have learned from other scholars. This is not always the end of the world, but it does help to know what original insights you have from working directly with the primary texts. Remember: at this stage, very early on in the process, it's okay to be wrong! You may discover later on that your thoughts were way off. That's okay. Your early notes here are inklings, a kind of "brainstorming" phase of research.

Here's a tip: Be sure to label clearly in your notes your own thoughts (vs. notes based on secondary scholarship). To make this easier for me, at the beginning of a section of personal thoughts, I put my own initials (NKG). That way, when I go back to these notes a week, a month, or a year later, I will know that these were my own thoughts and insights, rather than something I jotted down from another scholar.

Step 2: Discover

So, step (1) involves collecting and studying primary texts. Make that a high priority habit of research. Step (2) is the stage where I recommend you write up a bibliography for your research. A bibliography is a list of titles and other essential information for scholarship that you consider relevant to your research. Before we get too far into the "how" of finding relevant scholarship, I want to mention that sometimes I do Step (1) and Step (2) concurrently. That is because it often takes time to order books and other items through interlibrary loan, online bookstores, or to get it from a friend. So you might identify and order/request items, and at the same time start working through your primary texts. This kind of juggling is completely normal for academics.

I have a term I use for this second stage of research: *Blitzkrieg*. The goal is to go out there and find as much relevant scholarship as I can possibly find on my subject, more than even what I could read and use. And I put a lot of energy into identifying and collecting (e.g., PDF download) scholarship until I have a large library of material in hand. Now, I don't do a lot of "reading" of scholarship at this stage. I am just in "collecting mode." I might skim through things to see whether a resource is useful and relevant. I might read a bit of it out of curiosity. But the focus is on acquisition. That is because I like to work step-by-step. Step (2): collect, *then* Step (3): study. But maybe you are more of the kind of person that wants to read things as they come. The only complication with that is that ordered items don't always arrive in a timely manner, frustrating that sort of "as you go" style of research. Let's say you are studying Luke and Acts. You might want to study Luke first, but some of the Acts scholarship is more readily available. That complicates studying things as you encounter them. Do whatever works for you, of course, but for those of you starting out in research and wanting to try my system, I recommend focusing on just collection at this stage.

Now, when it comes to *how* to find bibliographic items, we are going to tackle that in the next chapter (chapter 3), so hang on until then when we get into the "Nuts and Bolts" of research and note-taking. But a question I do want to address here is how much scholarship to collect. I can definitely tell you what *not* to do. If your professor gives a minimum expectation of ten sources, that doesn't mean you *just* look for ten sources. If you are expected to engage with ten good pieces of scholarship, then at the *Blitzkrieg* stage I would recommend looking for three to five times the amount. So, a ten-source paper would have a thirty- to fifty-item initial bibliography. There is a simple reason for this: a lot of scholarship that you might think is relevant at first, turns out to be redundant, unhelpful, off-topic, etc. And perhaps some items are unavailable. At this stage, you cast the net wide, as wide as you can manage, and then you are in a good position to narrow it down to the most useful items. If you only start with ten, you might end up with only a few *truly* useful pieces of scholarship with which to engage. That's not the right way to go about it, so go big on bibliography. In the next chapter, I will give some advice on how to narrow your big bibliography down to the most important items as you research.

So just to reiterate this point, let's say you are writing an academic article. There's no real rule for how much scholarship to look at. Some types of articles might end up citing seventy items. Others, more like thirty. I know from a reviewer's end, we are never counting sources. But at the same time, it can feel like an article is "light" on engagement with current scholarship; or, alternatively, some scholars can come across overdoing it on dense, esoteric footnotes that interrupt the flow of the main text. It is helpful to err on the side of "too much" and then whittle it down with counsel from peer feedback.

Students sometimes ask me for a general rule of thumb for an initial bibliography. I hesitate to offer one because every writing project is different, topics have different expectations and needs, but just to give a very rough ballpark:

Academic Paper: aim for 50 bibliographic items

Academic Article: aim for 75–100 bibliographic items

Academic Book: aim for 100–200 bibliographic items

Now, those numbers might sound like a lot. But when you start researching, it's not hard to find bibliography items. The *hard* part is narrowing it down to the most important things to actually read. And keep in mind, you are not going to read and cite all of the things you identify and collect. The initial bibliography is just the bigger "library" from which you will determine what is going to be most helpful for you to engage.

Something important to mention here as you think about what to collect and read for your research: *be mindful of your own bias.* For most people, we gravitate towards reading what we want to read, especially the scholarship in our own ideological circles. But a good researcher casts the net wider and reads outside their own circles to challenge their thinking and open up the conversation.

Now, you can't read everything, obviously, so how do you make sure you are reading good material outside your circles? For me, the easiest thing to do is ask friends and colleagues for reading recommendations, especially those who work in different social, political, geographic, and ideological spheres. Now, some of you might be thinking *why is it important to read work from other kinds of scholars and scholarship?* My belief is that one of the beautiful things about academic study is what my friend A. J. Swoboda calls "serendipitous learning." You might call this "accidental" learning. In so many cases in my life, I order a book or article, not expecting anything important from it and—WHAM!—it is paradigm shifting for me. Reading outside of your circles sometimes (often?) has that effect because, as they say, "you don't know what you don't know." These exercises force you to see the subject from another perspective, in a foreign language or culture, or using a unique method or approach. All kinds of new and interesting things are injected into your thoughts. So, what harm can it do? There is an old myth, I call it the myth of "contamination." It's this idea that if you read something that you disagree with—and you find yourself appreciating a tiny little part of it—you will get infected with its cooties. But this myth comes from a place of fear and, honestly, stupidity. Only a fool believes everything they read. Read broadly, read "the other side," read "the wrong view," and be a learner. Having a solid education and a good head on your shoulders should supply you with enough confidence to say, *I can read stuff from all over the place and pick up something helpful or interesting, and skip over things I don't find compelling or convincing.* If you look at scholarship with *that* attitude, I promise you you just might learn something new.

Step 3: Study (Secondary)

My third step involves actually studying the secondary literature (and other primary literature) that you have collected. Chapter 4 will include all my tips and tricks for writing notes. So right now I just want to talk about the big picture of how to think about this process. The most obvious thing that shouldn't need to be stated is still worth saying: you actually *need* to have an information collection system. When I was a graduate student, I have to confess that my approach was pretty haphazard. I'd scribble digital notes here and there, but then later on I couldn't figure out where I had put some of them. In a panic, I would search my computer files desperately trying different keywords to figure out where I had saved my latest notes. It took me too long to come up with a better system where I could find my notes quickly and easily.

So, how to go about reading the scholarship? There are different ways of studying scholarship based on your personality and preferences. One method would be to sit down and read a whole book, and then go back through and jot down notes. Some people do that, if that works for you, go for it. As for me, after I look at the table of contents to see how helpful the book might be, and I skim the book to identify key areas of importance for my research, I like to write notes *while* I read the work. Oftentimes, I have thoughts while I am reading, and if I wait until later to jot down notes, I will forget what I was thinking. I gotta do it when it's first in my head.

My big advice for this stage is this: write lots of notes, because it's always better to have more material to work with than less, and you never know when and how you might use those notes again later (e.g., for a lecture, another writing project, a sermon, etc.). Let's say you order an article from interlibrary loan (ILL), and you get it as a scanned PDF. You read parts of it and decide that it's not relevant to your work. In the past, I might just delete it or forget about it. But maybe five years later I start working on a project where now that article *is* helpful—but I didn't bother to save it somewhere where I would easily find it again. That might sound like a one-off scenario, but it seems like it happens to me all the time. So now if I get a book from ILL, even if it becomes apparent that it is not going to be that useful for my research *on this occasion*, I might jot down some quick notes on it—basic ideas and arguments, etc. Or I might take a picture of the Table of Contents if that information is hard to find on the internet.

The wider goal of this step (3) is to have an extensive set of notes based on working with primary and secondary texts. Some of the notes will be facts, ideas, and quotes from the secondary scholarship. Some of the notes will be my own inklings, insights, ideas, and information. For book projects, I might have a notes file on my computer that is 150–200 pages long! That's because I want lots of material from which I will draw in order to support my work. In the end, I won't use some of the material, that's inevitable. But that's the nature of research, that's part of the process. Once you sit down to write a draft, you need to decide what will work best in the manuscript. And lots of information hits the "cutting room floor," so to speak.

Step 4: Analyze (Notes)

Okay, if you have reached this step in the process, you have lots and lots of notes, but it can feel like a big garbage heap of material, in my case often clumsily thrown together into a document. The digital version of a bunch of crumpled up Post-it notes shoved into my pocket. Again, I might have a notes file that is over a hundred pages long. If you are a "neat" person, you might have organized all the material as you went along. So, maybe you combine Steps (3) and (4). It makes sense. Believe me, I've tried that, and it just doesn't work for me. Whatever the case, for me this fourth step is about organizing and analyzing my notes and ideas so that I can start to gain traction on a set of big ideas, lines of evidence for my ideas, and perhaps also a linear flow of argumentation.

How should you organize your notes? I tend to organize topically. Let's say I am looking at the theme "peace." I might have a set of notes under the heading "Peace language in Second Temple Jewish Literature." Major sections should be labeled in such a way that it is clear as you scroll through a document where specific notes are located. More specific app/software information appears in the next chapter.

As you organize your notes, now is also the time to start processing the information you have collected to see where the "gaps" are in terms of scholarship, or where you see "pressure points" in the academic conversation, where you feel drawn to make a specific contribution. Ask yourself questions like: *Are there assumptions made by scholars that need to be tested? Are there clear gaps in knowledge or engagement? Is there a contingency of scholarship that has misread or misjudged primary information?* You will want to make another round of notes in your file(s) offering your latest thoughts (maybe in a different color, and make sure to clarify that these are *your* fresh thoughts). Again, get in the habit of writing your thoughts down *in the moment* rather than assuming you will remember later. Sometimes, I have had to table a project for six months or a year (unexpectedly)—I won't remember later what reactions, reflections, and thoughts I had "back then" unless I write them out specifically. Sometimes, my analytical notes are guesses, hunches, inklings, or feelings. I now write all of these things down because the analysis is fresh in my mind. I have learned that the "me" six months from now gets really upset at the "now" me if I am lazy and I don't record all my fresh thoughts. Otherwise, I have to do the analysis over again.

Part of the analysis process for me is revisiting my NPO (Need, Problem, Opportunity). When you first craft your NPO, you are kind of guessing at the "gap" in scholarship. You may have done some initial digging and "soundings" in scholarship, but once you reach this stage ("Analyze") ideally you will have worked through the most relevant and influential scholarship. So now is a good time to adjust or tweak your NPO. In most cases, it doesn't mean *scrapping* the NPO. If you notice some scholars have already done the work you are wanting to do, is there room for you to put a twist on the subject? Look at it from another angle? Bring in another conversation partner? Again, in almost all cases, there is still a way to make a contribution, you just have to find the angle.

It is also at this stage where you might want to write out your thesis statement, your *big idea* that drives your project. Look through your notes to see if other scholars are saying the same thing. If there is *no one* (or or very few), that is a positive sign that you have plenty of space to add to the conversation. If there are *lots* of scholars or scholarship proposing or supporting your thesis idea, then you need to adjust or tweak. Remember, a good thesis idea for most kinds of academic scholarship offers a fine balance of originality (something new to offer) and plausibility/support (evidence and argumentation that reinforces and backs up your idea).

Step 5: Outline (Draft)

Now is the time when I begin to do some writing of my own. Again, everyone writes according to their own personality and preferences. But as for me, I start with a large-scale outlining of the manuscript towards a first draft. I "chunk out" the whole project into its big pieces. For a book, that might be chapters. For an article or essay, I will create major section headings. At this stage, the titles of those headings are basic, kind of like "placeholders." That is to say, nothing is set in stone, they just help you with a bird's-eye view of the essay as you glance at the whole run of headings. I will also pop in rough word counts for each section. That way, I can step back and get a sense for evenness of the work. You don't want to spend a whole bunch of the allotted word count on the early chapters and then have to rush through later sections. Also, you don't want to get into the bind of going way over your allotted word count. Professors, editors, publishers, they care about the word count, they don't want to read something several times the expected length. So, it pays to map out the essay at the very beginning of your drafting process. Resist the impulse to just *start writing*. Sometimes you have nervous energy and thoughts and ideas, and you just want to *write*. That's fine, you can do that in your notes document (and later copy/paste to draft), or you can go ahead and do some of that in your manuscript. But for me, outlining the manuscript with section headings keeps me on track, writing evenly, knowing when to stop and move on to the next section, and it gives me smaller targets to aim for as I try to tackle the writing one section at a time.

Let's talk briefly about a book, a *long* project. Here, I still think it is helpful to sketch out the *whole* book. Now, when I say that, it is also knowing that after I write a chapter or two, I might revise the trajectory, ordering, or some of the topics of the book as I fine-tune the flow and argumentation. For my part, I tend to create separate files for each chapter of a book, but I might have one document that has the outline and flow for the whole thing and I use that as a kind of guide or TOC. The chapter files have target word counts (fuzzy and flexible) and will have section headings as I have explained above.

Step 6: Fill (Draft)

So now you have a manuscript file (or set of files) with section headings that outline the flow of the work (keeping in mind all of this is open to tweaks, changes, and reshaping as you write, revise, and rethink). The next step for me is aligning data from my notes document to pick what I want to "say" in the manuscript. So, you are *filling in* the manuscript with "notes information" in somewhat raw form, so that you have substance to work with as you do the actual writing (Step 7). Now, I can see two ways of doing this, and I have tried both ways over the years; they each have their strengths and weaknesses.

Notes in the manuscript. One approach is to copy and paste information from the notes document to the manuscript (which now has section headings). I put relevant "notes and quotes" (key quotations from primary and secondary literature) directly into individual sections. That way, when I am doing the draft writing, I can look down and draw off of those notes. If you take this approach, I recommend putting the "notes and quotes" in a special color, so you can easily distinguish them from the draft writing at a glance. So, I might choose blue or green for the notes.

Parallel notes. A second approach would be to leave notes in your notes file and work with side-by-side windows to draw from your notes. In this case, you would not copy/paste notes into the manuscript, but just have the notes file open as you write your draft document. For some people, the advantage of this system is that the manuscript document is neat, clean, and free of notes—it's just for the writing draft. The challenge here is that you always have to open two documents and the notes document would need to be organized in such a way that it is easy to draw from the notes per section. When I use this system, I prefer having two computer screens in front of me—something I can do easily in my home office, but not as conveniently when I am at a coffee shop.

Whichever system seems more beneficial, in either case, I find it helpful to have section-specific notes ready at hand as I write. This frees me up at the writing stage (Step 7) to *just write*. When I follow these steps, I don't have to go back to collect or analyze, I can just write. Now, of course research in real life is messy, so these steps won't always work out perfectly. But for the most part, when I get to the writing stage, I like to spend my time writing so that I can stay focused on linear and clear flow of argument and thoughts.

Step 7: Version 1 (Draft)

Step (7), in my process, is the beginning of the writing phase, where my own thoughts, ideas, and arguments are expressed. Some people say, "don't start with the introduction," because that is best done at a later stage of writing once you see the work really take shape and then are in the best position to "frame" the work. True, I agree with the gist of that. But I find that doing a little bit of "introduction-ing" helps to prime the writing pump. Sometimes, the stress of starting a draft can lead to writer's block—we will talk more in detail about that later. Just know that this is *only* a draft, and no one else needs to see the work in this form. Think about a sculptor starting out with just a lump of clay. This draft is your lump where you just want to start the shaping.

In my mind, a draft is a first attempt to get your main ideas and arguments on paper in one place. If you follow my system, by now section titles serve as your "way points." They will keep you on target. I often start at the beginning or towards the beginning and work my way through the sections, drawing from my notes (and then deleting the notes from the manuscript if I followed the *notes in the manuscript* approach of Step 6).

At this stage, I just write, without doing a lot in terms of footnotes. Now, when I quote or engage with a piece of scholarship, of course I will add a footnote. But I don't fill in all the information in the footnote, just because I have the goal at this stage of getting the main content in the manuscript. But I *do* recommend putting some key information in footnotes, like the author, some indicator of the title of the work, and page number. Some of the other stuff (publisher, city, year) can be filled in later in step (8). This is important: if I don't add this key information in the footnote right away (step 7), then I sometimes find that I just can't figure out what that source was. *And that's a disaster!* Yes, ideally it is in your notes, that's the way it should work, but sometimes I use the same author (or author's last name) a lot, and I didn't do a good job of labeling which source of theirs I am quoting. Do yourself a favor early in your systems of research and writing: *clearly label your sources with key bibliographic information and when you pull quotes from sources, make sure you note page number and the specific source.* On more than one occasion, I had to go back and figure out which exact source a quote came from. It's a pain—a preventable pain—that you don't want at this stage. You want the work done in the earlier stages to set you up for freedom at this stage to *just write*.[2]

I want to talk a little bit about *writing tone* as we think about the work we do in drafting the manuscript. There are two extremes you want to avoid. On the one hand, some writers make their arguments and engage with opposing scholarship like a raging rhinoceros. They bludgeon you with harsh rhetoric and make you (the reader) feel evil or stupid for not buying their arguments. On the other side, you have an overly apologetic

---

2. In the next chapter, we will address helpful apps and programs like bibliography management software. You can avoid a lot of footnote citation problems by utilizing automatic citations through programs like Zotero or Endnote.

meekness. The writing is full of "maybes" and "perhaps" and "I wonder." It is good to write with a dash of humility, but if the writing lacks drive, it can be underwhelming and you run the risk of losing the reader's interest. Aim for a space in between meekness and rage, the shy mouse and the charging rhino.

I remember when I was first applying for jobs, I sent around my CV (Curriculum Vitae, i.e., academic resume) and cover letter to some mentors. I recall James (aka, "Jimmy") Dunn giving me this advice: *in your cover letter, toot your horn softly, and then let your resume and references impress them*. In a polite way, he was telling me I was coming on too strong in my cover letter, I was blasting my horn in their ears. I needed to find a more subtle way to warm the reader over to offering me an interview. Writing a book is not exactly the same as a cover letter, but I think you get the point: tone matters. Most readers can sense when a writer is setting up a "straw-man argument" or treating opposing scholarship unfairly.

On the other hand, I often get seminary papers where students are afraid to assert their view. They will say "I think" or "I believe," or (worst of all!) "My opinion is." And every time I tell them, *just argue for what you think is right, provide evidence, and let the reader decide whether they are convinced*. These hesitations and needless qualifications tend to erode our authorial voice. Similarly, sometimes I read student papers where they just summarize and quote the views of scholars and never assert their own views. This makes the student a sort of editor or mediator stringing together scholarly ideas or quotes, like putting pearls on a string. One way to help avoid this is to spend time in your drafting phase writing down your own thoughts, and then adding scholarly quotes later on to support and supplement your own discussion.

Here's a tip: In the drafting stage, there are occasions where I leave a code in a place where I don't have exact information. For example, let's say I want to refer back to a certain set of pages in the book, but I won't have those exact page numbers until the publisher has produced the page proofs. So, at the draft stage, I use the symbol ### to mark places to change later. The reason I use that particular symbol is because it is easy to search for in the document later. I can do a text search that won't conflict with other symbols. I might use ### for spaces where I haven't completed bibliographic information. You can use any rare symbol that you like.

Step 8: Version 2 (Complete)

Step (8) is where I revise and complete the manuscript. So, during the drafting phase (step 7), I might leave footnotes with only basic bibliographic references. Or, I might leave a note for myself to add a bit of extra material on [X] in a specific part of the book. Maybe, in the course of drafting I realize I need to do a little bit more research. While I am drafting (step 7), I generally don't go back and do more research. My goal is to just get the bulk of the ideas and arguments down on paper (or screen!). So, in step (8), I fill in the manuscript with finishing details that I left out before. So, again, using our sculptor's image, if step (7) involves shaping the clay into the form of a person, then step (8) is getting more details with the figure's pose, muscles, clothing, hairstyle, etc. Typically, I don't do research at this stage. I just enhance what I have already written.

This is a really fun stage for me, because a lot of the "stressful" work is behind me. I have done the bulk of research, and now it is a matter of just strengthening and "finishing" what I have done. The type of work involved at this stage is pretty straightforward. Throughout the drafting stage (step 7), I will have left little placeholders here and there. Sometimes I write "DC" next to some information. "DC" is my shorthand for "doublecheck" information I am citing. This is a note that reminds me to follow up after I have finished the draft. When I am in drafting mode, I aim to write the bulk of the chapter or essay free from anything that is going to bog me down. So, with step 8, I go back as part of a kind of "clean-up" crew to tidy up the document, to move it towards completion. So, footnote references get fully cited, ancient reference abbreviations are checked, and I start to compile the book bibliography as well.

Step 9: Version 3 (Finalize)

The last major step in my writing process is a third runthrough of the manuscript, which I sometimes call a "perfect read." The goal of this step (9) is to iron out any wrinkles and smooth out the language (looking for typos and awkward grammar). Often I will print out the manuscript and read the text out loud with a red pen in hand to mark typos, small changes and edits, information that is still missing, and anything else that needs tweaking. The reason that I check the text this way is because when my brain (silently) "reads" the manuscript, it skips over common mistakes that I make. So, for example, I sometimes write "to" when I mean to write "the." And my brain doesn't always catch this when I reread my own writing silently in my head. I have found that when I read my own manuscript out loud, I catch about 90 percent of the awkward wording, typos, and bad grammar in my writing.

Now, I think some people are tempted to skip this stage. But I want to try and convince you that it is really important. I serve as an editor for many projects where I am reading other people's work before it goes to publication. And when I read an article, essay, or book full of typos, even if the content is really good, the writing still comes across as sloppy, even lazy. It is worth taking the extra time to go through the manuscript *one more time* to make sure it is a "clean manuscript," free of typos and errors.

Step 10: Engage (Feedback)

Now, if you have made it this far in the process, it would seem like you are done. And maybe in some cases that is true and you can send the document off to the editor or journal or publisher. But if you are willing and able, I recommend first soliciting feedback from your peers. Too often students—and even professional researchers—skip this step for one reason or another. For students, I am guessing it is because they are cutting it close to the deadline and can't wait to get feedback and revise. Or perhaps they are feeling embarrassed about their writing and worried what a peer might think. For professional researchers, we sometimes fail to solicit peer feedback because we don't really want advice from other people (*I know what I am talking about!*). Or, we might be running close to (or past!) a deadline. Or, there's always plain old laziness.

But I have attempted to get feedback on many (though not all) occasions, and it has *always* strengthened my work. Now, maybe I got lots of helpful feedback and it's a game changer. A friend may spot some gaps in my methodology, or call me on a weak argument. Other times, I get little bits of wisdom and insight that help to refine my work. In any case, it is worth the extra step to solicit feedback. When asking for feedback, you might want to be specific with your friends and colleagues about what *kind* of engagement you want. For example, for one project, I asked friend #1 to give his take on certain chapters, and friend #2 on other chapters. I know their time is precious and they might not want to read the whole thing.

Step 11: Version 4 (Refine)

Okay, once I've received that peer feedback, I look again at my work and make adjustments. It should go without saying that you as the author get to decide how much of that feedback you want to incorporate. (It's different if it is coming from your editor, then it might be more of an *obligation*!). Step (11) is my final step, where I make the last changes that primarily come from feedback and make sure everything is in order. Then I send it off to the editor or publisher.

Now, in the "real world" of publication, that's definitely not the end of the process. Again, the editor might (probably will) have feedback and may require revisions. Or, the editor may send the work out for peer review and you get corrections and suggestions that way. Sometimes, it can feel tedious, like spending too much time perfecting a recipe. But in my experience over the years, the overall peer-review process is good and does its job at making the academic work stronger.

Pacing the Steps

How do you know how long to spend on each step of the process? When do you move on, in order to stay on track, even when you haven't done as much work as you would have liked? There is no magic formula for this. But it might be helpful to have a rough framework in mind.

Let's say you have 750 hours that you can dedicate to writing a book over three years. I might plan and pace out the steps like this (knowing that I will need to be flexible and shift some things along the way):

Study (Primary Literature): 150–200 hours (~20–27 percent)

Discover: 40 hours (~5 percent)

Study (Secondary Literature): 150–200 hours (~20–27 percent)

Analyze: 15 hours (~2 percent)

Outline: 15 hours (~2 percent)

Fill: 15 hours (~2 percent)

Draft: 250 hours (~33 percent)

Complete: 40 hours (~5 percent)

Finalize: 10 hours (~1 percent)

Engage/Refine:3 15 hours (incorporating peer feedback into the manuscript) (~2 percent)

As you can see, the most time-consuming periods of my approach are the study steps and the initial draft. When I devise a research schedule for a book, I make a guess as to how much time each step might take. This is important, because if you sign a contract with a publisher *before* starting the research, you will need to estimate when you can deliver the complete manuscript to the publisher. It is okay to be off by a week or two (or three), but it is frowned upon to submit the manuscript many months or a year late. The more experience you get in doing research and published writing, the better you will become at "guestimating" timeline and more precise completion dates.

Final Thoughts

So, that's a bird's-eye view of my research and writing process. What I like about following a linear process like this is that it helps to plan out the schedule of work, and I like to mentally check a to-do box when I finish a stage. Due to a compressed timeline or "on and off" access to scholarship, there are times when it is not possible or easy to follow a process rigidly. That's ok! But for those of you who are just starting out in discerning a research and writing process, I suggest you give this a shot once, and then adjust it towards your liking, convenience, and benefit with subsequent projects.

In this chapter, we gave an overview of my version of the research and writing process, from initial study all the way to final refining where you make sure all the i's are dotted and the t's are crossed. In the next chapter, we are going to cover some of the same ground as above, but instead of talking about theory and approach in the abstract, we will look at how I approach the "nuts and bolts" of research and note-taking. We will especially concentrate on Step 2 (discovering and acquiring secondary scholarship), Steps 3–4 (note-taking), and Step 5–7 (outlining and drafting).

---

3. Sometimes the time-consuming part of this step is simply giving your peers time to give feedback; I tend to give readers four to six weeks to get me their comments. That creates some deadtime where I might work up the final bibliography and write "frontmatter" sections like preface, acknowledgments, abbreviation list, etc.

3

The Nuts and Bolts of Research, Note-Taking, and Writing

IN THE LAST CHAPTER, we offered a sweeping overview of my research and writing process in eleven steps. It's a personalized strategy, borne out of experience, that draws from the basics of good scholarship—discern a problem or need, discover, analyze and process, write, revise, and revise some more. In this chapter, we will go back through some parts of the process, but with a view towards getting into specifics of tools and resources. So, to keep the sculpting analogy going, if the previous chapter was about seeing the lump of clay take shape into a defined body (from an observer's perspective, let's say), this chapter zooms in on what's in the sculptor's hands, the tools of the trade. All artists basically use the same kinds of tools, but each artist has their own preferences when it comes to the exact brand or type. The same goes for academic writers. We all use electronic databases, word-processing apps, websites, and software, but we also have our specific preferences when it comes to these. As you expect by now, I will walk you through *my* personal go-tos and favorites, and you can adjust and "take or leave" suggestions as we go.

Building Your Initial Bibliography

So, you sit down at your computer, excited about research, and start a new document called "initial bibliography." And then . . . what? How do you actually get started with a topical bibliography? My tendency is to start with a good Bible dictionary to get a bird's-eye view of the subject and the current scholarship. If you are a beginning master's student, and you want something *very* basic, I would recommend the *Eerdmans Dictionary of the Bible* or the *New Bible Dictionary*. However, because these resources are *so* short and basic (thousands of brief entries packed into one volume), you aren't going to get a lot of good leads on bibliography items. And if the dictionary you are using is old or outdated, correspondingly their recommended reading will be as well. So, I recommend the more robust academic Bible dictionaries that give more space to topics and also recommended reading. Here are a few of my "go-to" Bible dictionaries.

Anchor Bible Dictionary. Now published by Yale University Press, this set is the "industry standard" resource of critical scholarship offering six thousand entries across six large volumes. It was published in the 1990s, so the scholarship may be a bit outdated at times, but it is still hugely valuable and a widely used resource.

IVP "Black Dictionaries" Set. IVP Academic produced a massively popular set of dictionaries in the latter part of the twentieth century which is kind of an evangelical counterpart to the *Anchor Bible Dictionary* (though IVP's set is more affordable and aimed more at pastors and students than advanced researchers). IVP has begun revising their dictionaries for a new generation. So the *Dictionary of Jesus and the Gospels* (2nd edition) has already appeared (2018) and the *Dictionary of Paul and His Letters* (2nd edition) is slated for 2023.

The New Interpreter's Dictionary of the Bible. Theologically, this set of five volumes would fit somewhere between ABD and IVP's dictionaries as a kind of "mainline" set. The NIDB is closer to IVP in terms of level, aiming at students and pastors, but it is a more recently published set (completed 2009).

Two more recommendations: check out *Currents in Biblical Research* and *Old Testament Abstracts/New Testament Abstracts*. *CBR* offers "state of the conversation" articles on a wide variety of topics in biblical, ANE, and early Jewish and Greco-Roman world studies. Obviously, not every subject imaginable is covered—the above dictionaries cover more breadth. But it's worth checking to see *if* there is an article on your subject of interest. The *NTA/OTA* periodicals provide 50,000+ abstracts of books, essays, and articles. These are like short summaries of individual pieces of scholarship. These

English abstracts are especially handy for foreign language articles to help you decide whether or not the article is worth translating in full.

Blitzkrieg Research (Step 2)

Now, let's say it is time to find *everything* you want to read in secondary literature on your subject. Obviously, it's impossible to read *every single thing* for most topics. But my recommendation is to cast the net as wide as possible at this stage, discovering more than you could possibly read. That massive bibliography will become the "menu" from which you choose the most relevant and most important items for your research. How much of that complete bibliography you actually read and use depends on a few factors: (1) type of research goal (essay? book?), (2) audience and impact (more technical? Or student level?), and (3) time. But as generic advice, I still recommend, at this stage of research, creating as large and complete of a *Blitzkrieg* bibliography as you can. That will provide you with the most material to discern that shorter list you will actually read—and, you never know when you will do research on the subject again, so you just might be doing yourself a favor for the future. This is one of those lessons I have learned over the years: do that little bit of extra work *now* by documenting and saving things that might not *seem* relevant or useful in the moment, because it may come in handy later.

First things first: where do I write down my *Blitzkrieg* bibliography? I use Google Docs (see below) and I work up a master bibliography for a whole project in one document. You will want something that is easy to use, you can access and pull up quickly (even on your phone), and that is searchable.

Okay, now we talk about where to find your secondary literature bibliographic items. It helps me to think in terms of "short sources" (essays and academic articles) and "books." Why? Because some research platforms cater to one category over the other and vice versa. Let's start with books.

Finding Books

An important place to start is crafting a set of keywords to search for in databases. Let's say you are studying "holiness" in the Bible. You need to have a cluster of related keywords, like "consecration," "sacred," and "purity." You might need to get more specific and look for holiness in "the historical books" or "the Gospels." Once you have identified that cluster, you will try them out in specific databases and websites. But let's say right off the bat, it doesn't help to just "Google" your keywords. That's gonna give you lots of unhelpful material and only a few (good, peer-reviewed academic) works at best. Here is where I start: my own institutional library's catalog.

Assuming you are a student at an academic institution, it's sensible to commence with your own library collection. Try out your keyword terms in a search, but look for a designated "advanced search" field labeled "keywords" (or something like that). If that yields too many results (including unhelpful items), you can try just searching in the "title" field. Research is *all* about experimenting, trying little tweaks and adjustments on wording and using different types of search fields. Now, your library may be massive and have lots of relevant material in terms of books—lucky you! Many libraries, though, have small holdings (as library budgets get smaller and smaller), so books might need to be ordered through a local consortium or interlibrary loan.

Any given institutional library is at the mercy of the online catalog software. Some libraries use a sophisticated search engine that helps students discover relevant material easily and efficiently. Other online catalogs are not as robust. I have worked at institutions across this spectrum. So, it's helpful to utilize good library catalogs at other institutions, even if you are not a student there! Now, keep in mind, you can't check out books from other libraries (unless you have some kind of institutional partnership or the library allows access for local residents), but it is helpful to use their online catalogs to build your *Blitzkrieg* bibliography. Here are a few that I use for research.

Tyndale House (UK) Catalog.[1] Tyndale House is a private and independent library in Cambridge (UK) focused on biblical studies. Scholars can travel to Tyndale House and spend a period of time there using their extensive collection of academic books and resources. I've been there many times and it is an extraordinary place to get a lot of "hard to find" items in one place at one time. They don't have *everything*, but they're probably as close as you can get to finding the most relevant items for research in one place in biblical studies. Now, not everyone can make their way to Cambridge for a visit to this incredible library. But their online catalog is able to be used by anyone, anywhere for the purposes of bibliographic research. You can't

---

1. http://tyndale.cirqahosting.com/.

check items out of Tyndale House—even people *in* the library can't check items out, they are for in-house research only—but you can discover plenty of titles worth buying or lending locally.

Why use the Tyndale House catalog? Because they have such a large collection of books, their catalog can search that massive collection to help you find many of the most important items for your research. The bottom line is this: a big library is going to have an online catalog that can search that library. So, find a big library (relevant to your field), go to their catalog, and see what you find. It's free and always worth exploring.

Harvard Hollis Catalog.[2] Speaking of big libraries—Harvard University has a pretty big library. When I was a student in Massachusetts (Gordon-Conwell Theological Seminary), I had a couple of opportunities to visit the Hollis Library. It is definitely a thing to behold. We are talking twenty *million* volumes. Unless you are a Harvard student, staff, or faculty (or affiliated through a consortium), you can't just walk right in, browse around, and borrow books. So don't book a flight to Cambridge, UK (Tyndale House) or Cambridge, MA (Harvard University) and say "Nijay sent me to borrow books." *But*—you *can* utilize their catalogs for research for free. And I do, all the time. So, try it out, you have nothing to lose (except a bit of time). Use your keywords and see if anything useful comes up that you didn't notice through other catalog searches. And you can try this out at other institutions, like Princeton Theological Seminary, Fuller Theological Seminary, Emory University (etc.), basically anywhere where you think there might be a large collection of works in your field.

Worldcat.org. I want to put another crucial resource on your radar. Worldcat is "the world's largest network of library content and services." This is a one-stop shop for searching all the catalogs of participating institutional libraries across the world. These are primarily academic libraries (not public libraries). There are (3) main benefits for using Worldcat for research. First, they combine multiple libraries to create a "super-search." Second, they tell you where you can find the book you are looking for (based on the zipcode you enter). If your own institutional library doesn't have the book, it might be at a library within driving distance.[3] The third major benefit of

---

2. https://library.harvard.edu/services-tools/hollis.

3. Let's say you drive an hour to that library where the book can be found; it could be the case that you can't actually lend the book, but I have found that if I can enter the library as a community member, and I can pull the book off the shelf, then I can read

using Worldcat is its indexing of editions and versions of a book. Let's say you want to look up the first edition of an academic book, or find the original German edition of an English translation. Worldcat does a good job of tracking editions and chronicling first, second, third (and so forth) as well as translations into other languages. This has come in handy many times when I have borrowed a book (ILL), sent it back, and realized later that I forgot to write down the complete bibliographic information. In almost all cases for a book, Worldcat has that information.

Google Books and *Amazon*. I want to recommend these platforms for research, but they have limitations and should be used with *caution*. So, if you go to https://books.google.com/, the search engine giant offers previews of thousands of books. You can try a general search of their index of books and see what comes up. It's going to be very hit or miss, but since it's free it's worth a try. Use this cautiously, because you might find a helpful book, but you only get a look at a few pages. In that case, order the book from a library or buy it. It is dangerous to "do research" reading only small previews of select chapters. It is best used to clue you into items you might want to order. Every now and again, if I am in a pinch, I might see if they have the relevant pages viewable for a commentary I need to consult. If I am able to see the exact page I need, then I feel more comfortable using it.

Amazon is also a decent place to search for relevant books, but it doesn't have a sophisticated "advanced search" set of features like library catalogs. Still, they sell millions of books, so it might be worth a search to see what comes up. And, again, they allow a "sneak peek" for some books, so you might get a sense for whether a book would be useful to loan or purchase.

Ebook Library Subscription Services. There are a couple of companies that offer access to ebook libraries for individuals at a monthly or yearly subscription rate. If you are not linked to an academic institution as a faculty member, staff member, or student, and you don't live near a theological library, these might appeal to you to gain access to academic books conveniently. The first resource I would recommend is called Scribd.[4] Scribd is a "Netflix-style" digital subscription service for books. They have a massive library of books, including a good selection of titles in biblical studies (and

---

it there or scan relevant pages with a phone app. See below on mobile scanning apps I recommend.

4. https://try.scribd.com/.

theology, religion, history, etc.). Scribd does have a mobile app so you can read on your phone or tablet. Another service is called Perlego.[5] Perlego is similar in structure to Scribd, but Perlego is focused on academic books. Again, if you find yourself struggling to obtain books either because of poor resources through your institutional library, or if you are researching independently, then these kinds of services may help you get what you need for a relatively small price. Scribd and Perlego partner with different publishers, so you might consider subscribing to both. You can run searches for free, just to see what is available in each app, and then decide. But then you will have to pay monthly/yearly to actually read the books.

Finding Articles and Essays

It is sometimes the case that searches for whole books on your subject of interest don't yield much. Or, you may have found some good material, but it is not as detailed as you would like. That is where more niche-focused academic articles and essays come into play. I find that for many of my seminary students, they seem content to reference biblical commentaries and biblical introductions, but these resources offer breadth, not depth. So, I challenge my students to make sure they are reading, utilizing, and interacting with academic articles and essays (and book-length monographs). But, again, sometimes writers wonder where to start to discover these shorter-form pieces of scholarship. For biblical studies, there are a handful of helpful databases and websites, but one of them is the industry standard: The ATLA databases (hosted by EBSCO).

ATLA Religion Database (EBSCO).[6] This is a database listing information for scholarship items in the areas of religion and theology. They index more than 460,000 books and 280,000 essays.[7] All that to say, scholars treat this as the most comprehensive database for biblical studies. You can search by title, Scripture citation tags, subjects/themes, author, and keywords. It is worth playing around and trying several of these options. If your search yields too many results (e.g., 8,000 items), you can set search filters like

---

5. https://www.perlego.com/home.

6. Biblical scholars love their acronyms! ATLA stands for "American Theological Library Association" which is responsible for this database; EBSCO is the hosting service, EBSCO is short for Elton Bryson Stephens Sr. (initials EBS) + CO (company).

7. https://www.ebsco.com/products/research-databases/atla-religion-database.

language (English only?), year (published after 1980?), or source type (journal article? essay?).

Once you find some helpful items, you can jot down the bibliographic information for the articles and essays to order through your library. But the ATLA Religion database also offers *some* items via direct PDF download. I have found that about half of the time, a PDF is immediately available. (Talk to your academic librarian about which journals you have full access to through their subscriptions.) Otherwise, I have to locate and obtain the item in some other way. If you are not currently a student, you might be able to get access through your alma mater (an option worth checking out). For non-students, you might be able to drive to a nearby college or seminary and use ATLA at a computer kiosk.

JSTOR Database. JSTOR[8] is another key database for discovering and obtaining journal articles. This database is not restricted to religion only, but covers dozens of disciplines and hundreds of journals. For example, I have benefited from access to journals in history, Classics, and social sciences. JSTOR is a repository, so items can be downloaded or read directly through the website. Again, institutional subscriptions are required for usage.

BiblicalStudies.org.uk. My hunch is that you will find 99 percent of what you are looking for in ATLA's and JSTOR's databases. But I do have a few other places I check just to make sure I've done my due diligence. One little online gem is a website called BiblicalStudies.org.uk, organized by librarian Rob Bradshaw. As far as I understand, Bradshaw tries to find older, out-of-print evangelical articles and books and indexes them, sometimes offering a PDF for immediate download. The content of his database is not comprehensive at all, but he does offer a lot and sometimes I find items there that I could not find anywhere else. As with all such free resources, no harm in looking!

SagePub and Other Publisher Websites. In the first quarter of the twenty-first century, academic publishers started realizing that instead of outsourcing journal access to JSTOR and other places, they could offer their own digital subscriptions or direct download of individual articles for a fee. For example, one of the largest and most important publishers of academic journals is Sage Publishing.[9] In some cases, if an article is not immediately

---

8. JSTOR is short for "journal storage," not a very creative abbreviation, but I never knew what JSTOR meant until I looked it up for this footnote!

9. https://us.sagepub.com/en-us/nam/home.

available for download through the ATLA database, you might have to log in directly to a website like Sage and access the article through your institution's subscription. Cambridge University Press and Oxford University Press have similar digital subscriptions. Keep in mind, though, that these subscriptions are not really designed for individual purchase. Through the publisher, in some cases, individuals *can* purchase a single article to download.

Academia.edu. This is a social-media networking website for academics. Professionals can upload documents to their profile page, including academic articles and essays (provided they have the proper permissions). If you find the name of an article or essay (through ATLA) and can't get ahold of the document itself, you might check to see if the author has posted it on their academia page.

Taking Notes (Steps 3 and 4)

How do you take notes? It seems pretty straightforward. You just write down things that you find helpful from your primary and secondary resources. But over the years, I have changed and refined where and how I take notes.

Google Docs (Google Documents). When I first began to do professional research (2006), I defaulted to using Microsoft Word, because that was the most common program at the time and the one I had the most experience using. Around 2014, I switched to Google Docs for a variety of reasons.[10] First, it's free. In the past, when I was a student, I benefited from getting Microsoft Office either free through my institution, or at a very reduced rate. Now, I don't have those benefits, and free is nice. Second, I use Google Drive to store all of my documents (more on that below). Google Docs works seamlessly with Google Drive. Third, if I ever "forget" where I put a Google Doc I created, it is very easy to use Google Drive to locate it. Finally, Google Docs has a very thorough search feature. Let's say I know that at some point in the past, I cited Morna Hooker, but I don't remember where. I can search Google Drive and it will easily bring up any document that has that name. Fourth, it works very well across devices, so I can pull up documents on my phone if I need to and edit from there. Finally—and

---

10. Although I talk about Google Workspace apps in this book, there are several companies that offer similar features and tools. It is worth exploring which ones fit your preferences the best.

perhaps my favorite feature of Google Docs—it is built for ease of collaboration. You can "share" a document with someone else, meaning that you can give them access to the link to your file. No more emailing a Word doc and going back and forth. In fact, Google Docs is a live, "editable," webpage so when your colleagues are co-writing or leaving comments, you can go on the document and *actually see them making edits in real time*. I have had times where I will go onto a Google Doc in class, and my students will go on as well, and we will write in the same document at the same time! When I have done collaboration this way, it has taken off the stress of trying to figure out which document is the most recent, and the headache of making sure I don't confuse that with other files. With Google Docs you just have the one file that continually gets updated. Moreover, Google saves versions automatically and you can revert back to an earlier version anytime you want. Let's say you accidentally erased a section and only discovered it days later. Google Docs can take you back to a version where that section existed and you can go from there. Each version that it saves is timestamped, so you can go back to any date in the past when you worked on the document and see what the document looked like back then. Here are the basics for how I set up my notes in a Google Doc.

First, my own technique is that I put all of my notes for a project in one document, rather than separate documents. That is for two main reasons: (a) it is convenient to have an all-in-one location for my notes on a project and (b) I find that when I am writing down notes from primary or secondary literature, that information might be relevant to multiple sections of my project, so it is nice not to have to switch between documents.

Second, I partition my Google Doc into sections that correspond to main topics or roughly into chapters that will become a book (or key sections of an essay or article). I would recommend using the "headings" feature in Google Docs to create these section titles. After you create all your section headings, you can ask Google Docs to create a hyperlinked "Table of Contents" (TOC) that will appear at the top of the document. Sometimes, I will end up with a notes document that is 200-pages long, and it would be tedious to scroll through the whole document to get to the section I want to work on. Using the hyperlinked TOC, I can just look for the section of interest (like in a book TOC) and click on it, and Google Docs will jump down to that section.

From there, I just put notes in under the relevant sections as I read. Sometimes, I create levels of subheadings, depending on the complexity and the detail of notes that need to be taken. In more recent years, I have made it a habit of putting a full bibliography at the very beginning of the main notes Google Doc, or at the end. Then, in the midst of my notes, I can make a brief parenthetical reference to mark where the idea or quote came from—e.g., (Dunn, *Theology of Paul*, 21).[11] I would just warn you to make sure you create a clear reference in your notes, so that you don't have to re-look up the note or quote later. Sometimes I have written down just the author and page, only to realize later I use multiple sources from the same author. Do that extra work when you take your initial notes so that you don't have to do the work again later when you are putting in full bibliographical details.

What kind of notes do I take in my Google Doc? About half of the time, I jot down the main ideas of the key secondary literature I am working with. I might also put in the abstract of the article or table of contents of a book. My general rule of thumb is to err on the side of putting *too much* information into my notes document, rather than *too little* information. Later on, you can always choose to ignore collected data or—if need be—erase it. Though I would rather keep it in case I use it later on for another project.[12]

I write down a lot of direct quotes in my notes. That is for a couple of reasons. First, I might use the quote itself in my writing (with proper attribution, of course). Second, if I have to leave the notes document dormant for a long time and return to research later, having the exact words of the author helps me refresh my memory better than any shorthand notes I might take myself.

Google Drive. As I mentioned above, I use both Google Docs and Google Drive. I write my notes (and manuscripts) in Google Docs and I save it all in Google Drive. Google Drive is free (for a certain amount of space, I pay a monthly fee now for more space). Google Drive lives in the cloud, which means it won't lose its data if my computer crashes. That also enables me

---

11. Be sure to mark clearly information from secondary sources versus your own thoughts and fresh ideas. There is a chance you could mistake another scholar's ideas for your own and commit plagiarism. We will talk about plagiarism more in detail later in chapter 4.

12. What about "orphaned" notes? Material that becomes irrelevant if a section is cut from the book but could be used in a later project? First, I tend to move that information to the bottom of the document as a kind of "junk drawer." In addition, I might copy and paste it into a document in a folder I label "Backburner" or "Future Ideas." Thanks to the sophisticated search intelligence of Google Drive, I don't worry too much about finding the information later.

to access my Google Drive on any device anywhere (e.g., a hotel business center if my device fails me). You can set up Google Drive so that it creates a folder system on your computer itself. Then you can access data as if it were your own computer folders and files.

Speaking of folders, within Google Drive, I keep all materials for one academic project in one folder. Within that folder, I have a few different items. One subfolder might be the book proposal. Another is the main notes Google Doc (see above). I often create a folder for documents associated with the publisher I am working with, such as their preferred ("house") academic style guide. Another document will eventually be the manuscript. And a subfolder will also contain all the digital pieces of scholarship I have collected. Many of these are PDFs of articles that I have downloaded from ATLA Database or other databases. Some PDFs may be scans of essays and book sections that I have requested from my library or scanned myself. I usually sort the PDFs into topical folders so that I can read and utilize them in stages. Within each topical folder I will have a sub folder named "Read" or "Done." When I have read or finished using a secondary scholarship document (article, essay, etc.), I drag it into the "Read" folder, so I know that I can move on to other documents.

One of the best features of Google's suite of apps is that Google Drive performs "OCR" on any PDFs in your drive. OCR stands for Optical Character Recognition. That means when you search for a key term in your drive, it can search not only word-processing documents like Google Docs, Microsoft Word, spreadsheets, Powerpoint/Keynote/Google Slides, but it also searches PDFs because it can "read" the words in the PDF. Not all computer search systems have that level of intelligence. This really comes in handy when you want to search all your PDFs for a topical term or author name. One caveat: Google's OCR sometimes has trouble with foreign languages, especially languages that don't use the traditional English language characters. So, searching in Koine Greek, Classical Hebrew, Aramaic is not as precise, so it won't yield perfectly accurate results. It also depends on how "clean" the scan was of the document that became the PDF. If the book page was bent or the scan image itself was blurry, this makes it much harder for the OCR system to know the difference between "m" and "r+n" (for example).

Google Keep. This is starting to feel like an advertisement for Google. I don't get paid any commission from Google! But I do like how cross-compatible many of the apps are. Google Keep is a "sticky notes" style of note-taking on your computer or mobile device. I don't take academic notes on Google Keep. It is not designed for lengthy notes. It is used for short notes and lists. For example, you might put your grocery list on there, or jot down a recipe. So, how does this help with academic research? I think of Google Drive and Google Docs as my "long-term memory" and Google Keep as my "short-term memory." If I am out and about, and I have an idea for my research, or I hear a good quote somewhere, I might jot it down on my phone in Google Keep. It is a nice place to return to easily for random information that you want to follow up on later, and then transfer it to the proper document.

Bibliography Management Software (Endnote, Mendeley, Zotero, etc.). In the same way I am zealous about using Google Docs, I have many friends who are passionate about the bibliography management software and apps that they use. Confession: I actually don't use these tools consistently. I know it is a timesaver and can make research more efficient, but I just haven't had the energy and motivation to sit down and learn how these programs work. What is bibliography management software (BMS)? BMS is designed to help you store, organize, and utilize bibliographic information. Let's say for a book project you read fifty books, thirty articles, and twenty essays. BMS can help store and organize that data all in one place. Furthermore, some BMS can track down the correct and complete bibliographic details for you, and may also cite any bibliographic item in your word-processing document directly in the citation style you prefer. Students sometimes ask me which BMS they should get. Having looked at the options over the years, I tend to recommend Zotero, mainly because it is free and offers all the main features that I have mentioned above.

Document Scanning App. Back in the *old* days, if you wanted to scan information from a book or journal, you had to take the book to a scanner (like a scanner on a copy machine). Back in the 1990s, I had a flatbed scanner—they were all the rage! But these clunky, often unreliable machines became virtually obsolete when smartphones came along with their high-quality cameras and intelligent processing apps. So, nowadays, I tell my students to invest in a good scanning app on their mobile phones. The basic idea is that you can take a picture with your phone and the scanning app will convert the image into a PDF. There are all kinds of specialty tools that these apps can apply, to brighten the image, "flatten" a curved page digitally, perform OCR on the image, and resize. Many such apps are free for basic features.

But it is worth paying a bit for benefits like automatic upload to Google Drive or DropBox. Currently, I use SwiftScan.

In this chapter, we have looked at resources, apps, and tools that can be helpful for the stages involving research and note-taking. The big picture is that it pays off in the long run to have good systems in place early in your writing career. Try some of the apps out (especially free ones), test out a few different tools. Maybe commit to trying one thing for six months and see how it goes. Another thing I want to mention here: *ask for help*. Utilize friendships in person and on social media to ask for advice and even a one-on-one tutorial. When I was learning about Logos and Accordance Bible Software, I asked "superusers" to meet one-on-one with me to show me their setup and answer questions. Their insights and walkthroughs have been invaluable.

In the next chapter, we will go deeper into the work of drafting and writing, producing your manuscript. Researching requires one set of skills and practices, writing clearly, effectively, and efficiently takes another set. Every writer is different, but there is some advice that helps out most people. Like anything else, some people are naturally good at it, and for others it takes work to improve. We will offer tips for both beginning writers and more advanced and experienced ones as well.

4

Best Practices for Manuscript Writing

Time to Write: Where to Begin?

I GET THIS QUESTION a lot from students. *Where do you start?* Sometimes new authors feel uneasy about the writing process, because it can seem daunting. Staring at a blank page can psych you out. *How am I ever going to finish this? Why did I agree to write this? Do I really have anything helpful to say?* There are two ways that I take a first step towards putting black letters on the white digital page. First, I process my big ideas and arguments. I don't tend to do this directly on my manuscript document. I either do this in my notes document, or I create an entirely separate document that I call "Big Ideas" (or something like that). In that "Big Ideas" document, I sketch my own ideas and arguments (after doing all the primary and secondary research). This is not only a great practical exercise to "know what I want to say," but it also gets the creative juices flowing for putting material in the manuscript document. Once you have a short summary of those "Big Ideas" and you can look at them, you can gain a bit of confidence that, yes, you *do* have something to say.

Second, I create section headings in the manuscript document with rough word counts. At this stage, the headings and word counts are just guesses. Think of it like "storyboarding." Filmmakers use a stack of sketches to visualize the arc of the movie through a series of mocked up images that depict key plot points. In the same way, I use headings as segments of a bigger project that keep me on track and help me visualize the whole. It helps me process the flow of the argument, and the word count targets ensure that there is balance. After that, I work through the manuscript, section by section, keeping an eye on the section word count. If I feel the need to go over word count (which inevitably happens every now and again), I can look ahead to where other things might need to be shifted.

Overcoming Writer's Block

Along with anxiety about where to begin, you can also have the challenge of writer's block, something that gets in the way of doing the writing itself. It might be fear and intimidation. It might be a sudden loss for words. I've been there, we've all been there, so what do you do? Don't overthink it, or over-psychologize it, that's probably just going to make it worse. There is a mantra I use with my students to help them overcome writer's block, and I hope it will help you as well: "Write something bad, and then make it better, until it's good." So, if you are worried about how to write something "good," then don't. Write something bad. Just. Write. The hardest step is often the first step, putting those letters and words on a page and starting the stage of "manuscripting." But if your "goal" is just to write—even writing something not great, *anyone can do that!* Just get some of your thoughts into words and go from there. Then, leave it. Take a break, have a little celebration. Eat some chocolate, take a nap, go for a run. Then you return and you go back over what you wrote and *make it better*. You don't erase it (unless it truly is garbage, sometimes that happens, that's okay too). You edit and reshape, and then you take a step back and say, "better." That process works for me. It's a small step that I make to push through the block. I know I can write something "bad," because I know later I am going to improve upon it.

Finding Your Writing Voice

Before you try to write a whole book, it is helpful to spend time learning about your writing "self" and finding your writing voice. What does that mean? Let's talk about the opposite. When I was a student, I was afraid of academic writing, because I didn't want to be "wrong." That would be embarrassing. So, I would "hide" behind the secondary scholarship. In my academic papers, I would showcase great ideas and quotes from various scholars. My work would be flooded with quotations and citations of scholarship. I thought that if I stuffed my writing with enough scholarship, I was unassailable. What I didn't realize is that, when I did that, "I" wasn't really there in the paper. I was like a host, bringing forward the thoughts of *other* people, other scholars. I allowed the voices of other scholars to drown out my own writing voice. That's not always bad. If you are summarizing the state of scholarship on a certain issue, it makes sense that you foreground the relevant material. But when it comes to a traditional book or article, the main voice should be the author's voice.

So, how do you do that? It begins, I would say, with making sure you have done enough research with the primary material that *you* have *your own* thoughts on the subject at hand. Don't just stitch together other people's thoughts. When it comes to manuscript writing, the way I have reinforced using my writing voice is by doing a lot of free-writing in the manuscript, articulating my thoughts and ideas, and then *later* putting in relevant quotes and content footnotes. In my approach to academic writing, I suggest letting the main text of your work put forward mostly your own ideas and arguments, adding in other voices for insight, nuance, and support.

Part of this for me is not letting footnotes get carried away. We all have seen academic books where the footnotes take up more of the page than the main text. On the surface, this can look really intelligent. But it has the danger of distracting the reader from tracking with *your* voice. All things being equal, footnotes are designed for citation of scholarship in a non-distracting way, and to comment on a related issue for "more information." It becomes problematic when that "more information" starts to take over. When you write a content footnote (where you do more than cite scholarship), ask yourself, "How important is this information for the reader to follow along with me in my argument?" If the content is not important, then you might ask yourself if it is necessary at all. Maybe it is, maybe it isn't. If it is *very* important, you might consider whether it actually belongs in the main text. Why relegate it to a footnote? My hunch is that content footnotes *feel* important in general, but add little or nothing to the main arguments. Whatever you decide to do, be aware of what purpose the footnote serves. Also, be prepared for an editor to weigh in!

The Writer

Use of "I/Me"
(Personal Language and Self-Reference in Scholarship)

When I was young, I was told not to use "I" or "we" language in academic writing. I think I get the idea behind that advice. We mustn't make our points from personal opinion, but from logical argumentations. That is a value I affirm and teach. But sometimes the use of personal language is hard to avoid. "In this article, it will be argued that . . . " That is just a roundabout way of saying "I will argue that . . . " There's no use in hiding it. The reader knows there is a real, fresh-and-blood human behind a keyboard somewhere writing the article. At the same time, an overuse of personal expression in certain kinds of academic writing can *over-personalize* the work. I offer two bits of advice on this. First, pay careful attention to the *level* of academic writing. A more popular level work, like a magazine article, is more comfortable with drawing out the author's persona in more explicit ways than an academic article or monograph. Second, note the *genre* of the writing. Some types of work are more personal, and some are less. If I am writing a dictionary entry (let's say for the *Anchor Bible Dictionary*), I am not going to use personal language. The entry is essentially "fact-driven" and requires a relaying of basic, current scholarship. The same goes for study notes in an academic study Bible (like the *HarperCollins Study Bible*). And I would expect most dissertations maintain that more traditional "objective" tone that discourages self-reference. Though this can be taken to an extreme. Once in a while, I will see a scholar refer to their own work in the third person: "Nijay Gupta has written a book . . . " I find that awkward and weird. I think it is perfectly fine to say "In my work on . . . " Again, the point of that would not be to pat yourself on the back for having written a book; you might genuinely want to make reference to more extensive arguments you have made elsewhere, or where you first offered evidence for a point. In that case, it seems appropriate.

But there are occasions where you might be writing something that allows for or encourages a more personal voice—notice how many times I have used "I" in this book and even this section! It all depends on the audience of the literature and expectations and dynamics of the genre. There are academic articles where I have consciously avoided self-reference as much as possible. And there are articles where it seems more appropriate, even expected. In the end, this is something to think about with your editors, and sometimes there is a personal style factor as well. My personality tends to gravitate toward a more autobiographical style of communication, but it might be different for others.

Sharpening "The Hook": Writing a Good Introduction

In chapter 1 we talked about how important it is to arrive at a clear and compelling problem. When you get to the writing phase, you need to "sell" the reader on that problem early on in the introduction. I recently read an editorial review of a journal article (where the reviewer rejected the article for publication). The reviewer's comments went something like this: *the article offers a lot of data, but it felt like a series of comments in want of a real and urgent problem. I found myself losing interest in the article after only a couple of pages, partially due to a lack of awareness of where the academic conversation began and where it was going.* That might sound harsh, it's never something you want to hear, but it is a real obstacle to successful writing. You need to know what the NPO is (again see chapter 1), and then you need to know how to "hook" the reader in your writing from the start. It's not enough just to begin, "In this book we will explore [X]." You need to confront the reader with the *why* from the outset. *Why is this topic important (now)? What problem or issue will it resolve? How does the problem affect the reader, such that they need to "read on" to find the solution?* Now, there is such a thing as "overselling" the problem. Most readers can sniff out exaggeration. But it doesn't take much to spend some time in the introduction trying to put your finger on the nagging problem that must be addressed. It doesn't necessarily need to be the solution to end worldwide hunger. For academic writing, it is natural for the problem (and solution) to involve problematic ideas that need correcting or nuancing, or gaps in thought that need to be filled.

On many occasions, good book publishers push authors on this. They want to ensure that they can "sell" the work and help the book find its audience. So, a book proposal will have some of these features built in: *what is the problem or need that is being addressed? Who is the audience for this book and what relationship do they have to this problem? What has already been published on this subject, and how will your work distinguish itself in the market?* If these questions and issues are hashed out at the beginning, it is much easier to write the introduction with this in mind.

What else should be included in a good introduction? I like to give the reader a sense for the main ideas and arguments, and where the book is going. You need to remember: most readers are lazy and distracted. They give up on books quickly. Sometimes they are reading multiple books simultaneously in the same week. They might skip around in an academic book or "skim." (By the way, I don't think "skimming" is lazy per se, I skim all the time, trying to find the most relevant material for my research.) So, introductions need to be crystal clear, compelling, and easy to read. Even if *eventually* your book will wade through technical information, I suggest making the *introduction* as accessible as possible—it might inspire an intimidated reader to press on. Readers (like me) will go back to introductions of books we have read to get a refresher if we want to reference the book. The introduction is like an opening scene of a movie: you have a small window of opportunity to warm your reader over and convince them that the time and energy of engaging in "the whole thing" is worth it in the end.

"Risk-Writing"

Academic writing is hard, let's be honest. Yes, the research itself is laborious and exhausting at times. Yes, the art of writing is a challenge. But it is difficult also because you are putting your work out there for consumption and criticism. Knowing that, there can be the temptation to do "safe-writing." Safe-writing is about *not* saying new things, particularly avoiding controversial statements, things that make you vulnerable to pushback. Especially in my student days, and if I am being honest also in my early career, I tried to tiptoe around sensitive subjects and stay in comfortable topic spaces where I could "hide" behind the scholarship of others. Safe-writing is risk-free precisely because I can feel unassailable by just repeating what other people have said and stay comfortably and confidently within "consensus" views. But the drawback of safe-writing is: it's boring, forgettable, and not academically generative.

Risk-writing, on the other hand, is the spirit that makes arguments (with supporting evidence!) that question assumptions, the status quo, and sparks fresh conversation. Risk-writing challenges the reader, and opens up new spaces for learning and intellectual growth. Risk-writing is exciting, inspiring, and generative. But it comes with . . . *risk*. You are putting your ideas out there, you are putting *yourself* out there, and that can be scary. But for most kinds of professional writing and writers, this *is* the space we live in. (Unless you write instruction booklets for kitchen appliances, then you have to be boring, sorry.) So, I want to push you: challenge yourself towards innovative approaches and fresh ideas, be willing to say new things and stand behind your work. That doesn't mean being controversial just for attention or to be "edgy." You really do need to have support for your ideas. But *good* writing grabs the reader. Put yourself out there and start an interesting conversation.

So, how do you practice "risk-writing"? When you are formulating your main ideas, that is the time when you ask yourself: *How am I pushing out beyond where others have gone?* There is a bit of a dance to this, because if you push too little, you are not really taking very much of a risk. If you push out too far, you don't really have solid ground (of evidence) supporting you. You have to stretch your ideas just enough that you *feel* that anxiety and vulnerability. Once you know what you want to say, you have to commit to that when you sit down and write the manuscript.

As I will mention below, it is important to have dialogue partners who give you feedback on your writing. If they are experts in the field, they can test your ideas and let you know if you have gone "too far" in terms of risk. Hopefully, they will also tell you if you didn't push far enough, if your writing comes across as "safe." If you are working with a publisher and editor(s), they will also give you feedback on your writing. Generally speaking, editors want solid writing that has thorough support, but obviously they also want engaging and inspiring scholarship that is generative and provokes reaction and ongoing dialogue. All that to say, do your best, be brave and take those risky steps in your writing, and then rely on colleagues to help you to ensure you are hitting the right level of risk.

Engaging with Other Scholars

In academic scholarship, it is inevitable that you will interact with the work of other scholars. There is, of course, the literature review chapter in the dissertation, but otherwise monographs, articles, and essays typically engage with relevant scholarship on a regular basis. So, it is helpful to consider *how* you interact with others. In the academy, "criticism" is normal, by which I mean intellectual disagreement which sometimes involves refuting the ideas and arguments of others. There is nothing wrong with that, it is common and expected in this environment. One of my friends refers to this as "crossing swords," and I find that an apt image.

But it really does matter *how* you engage with the work of others. There is a kind of *ad hominem* style of pushback that feels unprofessional and, to be honest, mean; a "hitting below the belt" style of argumentation. I remember very vividly an academic conference session where two scholars were *meant* to be engaging in respectful debate. They broadly represented two sides of an issue. The first speaker got up and gave a thoughtful, though predictable, defense of his view. The second speaker got up and absolutely stunned the audience by making numerous seemingly personal attacks against the person, character, and intelligence of the other scholar. Many of us in the audience were visibly uncomfortable. One or two people got up and left, I presume because they simply could not stomach listening to this anymore. I had some responsibilities for helping to plan the event, so I felt somewhat responsible for what felt like a disaster of a session. In fact, after the session, I immediately found the first speaker and apologized for the way he was treated. The next day, the board overseeing that session met, and we sat for a while in silence, speechless at what transpired. *How did this happen? Why would someone do that?*

I tell you this story, because that session is burned into my memory as a failure to create meaningful discussion. Hostile, "point-scoring" forms of academic discourse are a cancer to our collective work. That fateful session was more than a handful of years ago, and I fear the situation in modern scholarship has only gotten worse—now we have social media. I don't want to be one of those curmudgeons who rants about the evils of Twitter and Facebook. But numerous studies have shown how digital social media not just facilitate uncivil interaction, but inspire and promote it as well.[1] The bar on social media is set so low for respectful and patient dialogue, that any attempt at academic discussion is all but futile. The pandemic, it seems, amplified this problem, because in-person academic gatherings (where there is hope for more civil engagement) were put on hold. I am not an expert in all of the social psychology behind this phenomenon, but I have noticed an erosion of generosity when it comes to how we respond to those we disagree with.

A simple rule to follow, when it comes to interacting with others online, in print, or in person, is something I learned from sports: *play the ball, not the person.* In soccer, if you *try* to trip your opponent to make them lose the ball—that's a foul. So, focus on the ball. In our academic case, the "ball" is the discussion at hand. Focus your energy, your attention, and your

---

1. See the 2020 article Olaniran and Williams, "Social Media Effects."

arguments on breaking down the weaknesses in the *arguments* of "the other side." But there are some things that should be off-limits. Don't put into question the intelligence or integrity of other scholars. And don't make a "straw man" argument, where you refute an oversimplified and reductionistic version of the "other side." Your own arguments should be made on the basis of extensive and concrete evidence, *not* on making someone else look stupid or evil.

In fact, it is the responsibility of every scholar to show the highest level of integrity and generosity of spirit, and that involves giving credit where it is due. Even when you must be critical of the work of others—again, a natural and expected part of academic discussion—it is fair and right to point out the strengths of their work. This is a habit of mine that I developed when writing academic book reviews. There are very few books that I read where I agree *completely* with the work. So too, I don't read many books that I *completely* disagree with. And, in fact, the point of a review is not whether I agree with it or not, but that I can use my expertise to evaluate and engage with the main ideas and arguments of the book. So, in most cases and as relevant, I try to discern two or three *strengths* of a book and two or three *weaknesses*. This allows me to interface with the book with both a critical *and* generous spirit.

Recently, I read a helpful essay that promoted what the author called "intellectual hospitality."[2] Intellectual hospitality welcomes a diversity of thinkers to come together for mutual learning. The opposite is "intellectual war." This is the posture that seeks to make a stranger and enemy out of the other, and to destroy them. Cherie Harder offers helpful advice on how to foster intellectual hospitality in an often unwelcoming intellectual world.[3]

Read widely. Especially, read outside of your comfort zones and read with generosity and openness the works of those who don't live in your "camps."

Openness is not acceptance. Just because you read someone else's work seeking to learn doesn't mean you have to accept their ideas.

Pursue friendships with people who are different. We tend to stick to our groups where we feel comfortable. But venturing out to befriend others can deepen our empathy.

---

2. Harder, "Reviving Intellectual Hospitality."
3. I want to give credit to Harder for all of the points below, but the explanations and additions include some of my own thoughts and experiences.

Ask others if you treated them fairly. When you develop your counter-arguments against "the other side," reach out to them and ask if they feel their views and arguments were represented fairly. This seems to me to be a courtesy that we would want as well—good old Golden Rule!

Cultivate curiosity. To create a diverse, hospitable intellectual community requires genuine interest in the work of others. Again, the goal isn't acquiescence to the views of others, but true understanding and gracious empathy. Snap judgments and hostile reactions poison such opportunities.

Avoid unnecessary provocation. Before you post that comment, write that email, send that text—think to yourself, will this embarrass someone, hurt them, make them upset, and is it necessary for me to do so?

Talk about respect and charity at the outset. When you gather for discussion, or let's say you are planning a collection of essays. Talk directly and explicitly about the ethos of your group, and the values you hold of civility and listening. Establish a culture and spirit of "inquiry, generosity, and warmth" (Harder).

Invest in relationships, not just ideas. Try to see the intellectual task as an inherently social one. Don't just "argue," even though critical discourse is good and necessary. Come together with others towards deeper understanding. Harder talks about discourse as a "social act" where lives and ideas become entangled.

Be open to change. We can enter into dialogue with walls up and weapons prepared. Or we can step in with minds and hands open to learn. It is not a necessity to change one's mind in the midst of learning, but it *should* be a priority to be *open* to learning new things.

Inspire, don't overpower. In the midst of discussion, trying to overpower the other often backfires. It is better to make a case that *inspires* the other and invites them into understanding.

Frequent Summaries

One of my favorite features of good academic books is end-chapter summaries. Why? Readers are lazy. They get distracted. They start and stop books. They skip information. As much as we want readers to read every single word we have written carefully, the reality is—they don't. So, I think it is helpful to build in some "scaffolding" to help readers who need some aids to stay connected to the main arguments and flow of the book. Chapter summaries serve that purpose. To writers, frequent summaries can appear redundant and tedious. That is because we (writers) have been living in the book's ideas and content for months, perhaps years. We have already spent hours upon hours pondering and reflecting on the subject. But most readers are coming without that preparation. And in the midst of sometimes advanced academic discussion, they might get a bit lost. So summaries can ensure those kinds of readers are "keeping up" with the argument. It's also helpful to think about how other kinds of readers might use the book. You have someone who read your book "once upon a time" and later has reason to come back to it again. They are helped out by going to those summaries to refresh their memory. And there are some readers who never plan to read your book. They just want the highlights. Let's say they have only thirty minutes to look at your work, and then they will move on to the next research item. So, of course they will peruse the table of contents, introduction, and conclusion. But having frequent summaries will inspire some of these "perusers" to get a better sense of the main ideas and arguments in each chapter.

When I review books for a journal, I find chapter summaries a helpful indicator that I am "tracking" with the author. The writer wants the reader to follow them on an intellectual journey. These summaries are "checkpoints" to make sure readers are caught up. What I tell my students is that summaries don't have to be long to be effective. Even short summaries are better than no summaries!

Plagiarism: What Is It, and How to Avoid It

Hopefully by the time you read this book, you will have already had a higher education tutorial on plagiarism. Plagiarism is broadly defined as taking someone else's work or ideas and passing them off as your own. This is considered a form of theft and there are steep punishments for plagiarism, which may involve legal action. All that to say, you want to set yourself up well for avoiding it.

In my mind, there are two forms of plagiarism: intentional and unintentional. The intentional form is when a student or writer steals another person's research or work and passes it off as their own without acknowledgment, credit, or proper attribution. That is a serious crime and deserves a serious punishment. In my fifteen years of teaching, I have only seen intentional plagiarism happen once or twice.

Much more common is unintentional plagiarism. This happens when a writer takes notes on or acquires information from a piece of scholarship and then fails to cite that source of knowledge due to neglect or ignorance. Let me give an example. Many years ago, I assigned a group of freshman students to read a literary classic. I asked each of them to write a book review, identifying five themes from the book. When I sat down to look at the book reports, I was surprised to find that a group of about ten students had some of the same exact themes using some technical language I was sure they did not come up with on their own. So, I needed to interview each student to figure out the story behind this. What I learned was that this group of students had searched online for the Sparknotes summary of the book which includes the book's main themes. These students had copied down some of their themes from the Sparknotes website. Now, *getting* your themes from another source is not in itself wrong—I hadn't forbidden that, because it didn't really occur to me. What was *really* problematic was that they failed to *cite* the source for their theme ideas. And *that* is plagiarism. You see, in the minds of most of these students, plagiarism is when you copy and paste sections from someone else's work into your own word for word. Yes, that is plagiarism. But it is *also* plagiarism to take someone else's unique ideas and pass them off as your own, unless it is common knowledge.

Another way that someone commits unintentional plagiarism is by accidentally mixing up one's own ideas and notes with that of the second scholarship they have copied down. A relatively recent example of this involves a respected commentary writer who admits that he drew heavily from others' works without giving proper attribution.[4] I believe this can easily happen if you don't clearly identify which notes are ideas and wording from another scholar, and which are your own. Thus, in my notes documents, when I am doing "free thinking" and "free writing," I tend to label that section with my initials (NKG) to make it clear this is my own wording and ideas. And when I am summarizing the ideas of other scholars and jotting down their words, I try to clearly label their own material with their initials (e.g., BRG, or SGE).

---

4. See https://www.eerdmans.com/Pages/Item/59043/Commentary-Statement.aspx; see also https://blog.lexhampress.com/2016/09/19/2016919an-announcement-from-lexham-press-regarding-eec-james/.

One practice that can help you avoid any concerns about mixing your words with that of scholars in your notes is to make sure to write your manuscript in a completely different document than your notes. Then, when you write your manuscript, you will know it is all your own words. You can consult ideas and material from your notes document from there without worrying about getting mixed up.

One safeguard for any academic writer is to get into the habit of erring on the side of *overciting* their sources rather than *underciting* them. If you have too many citations acknowledging your sources, you can go through later and take some of them out if it seems cumbersome to cite the same source repeatedly. Or, you can leave the extra citations in and rely on your editor to tell you if and when some of those citations are unnecessary. There is a mantra I use with my students that I will talk about in more detail later, but comes into play here as well: "Quote sparingly, paraphrase often, cite always." The part "cite always" means making sure to give full credit whenever and wherever it is due, whether you are using a scholar's words or their ideas.

No Writer Is an Island: Create a Feedback System

The last thing I want to mention in this chapter on writing is the importance of creating a feedback loop *during* the writing stage. I must admit now that in the early years of my career, I didn't solicit feedback from my peers before sending out an article or book proposal. I think that I was too intimidated or embarrassed of what they might say. Perhaps I was lazy and didn't want to go back and incorporate feedback. But over the years, I have come to be convinced that it is actually a crucial part of growing as a scholar and ensuring long-term success. Early feedback on your work can identify weak points and blind spots. It is worth taking the extra time and effort to hear from colleagues about where there is lack of clarity, weakness in argumentation, and room for improvement. And, to be honest, it is also nice to hear some positives and words of encouragement from peers.

The process is not a complex. After I finish a book manuscript, I try to send it out to a few people, whom I ask for feedback. At first, this can be uncomfortable, because it is hard to hear negatives about your work from others, even (especially?) from friends. But I try to put it into perspective: they are giving their opinions and trying to help you. And at the end of the day, it is *your* work and you can choose to take their advice or not. There is some freedom in that. Now, when you are at the stage where your *editor* is giving feedback, you will need to work with them on how to take their comments seriously. But in the earlier stages of initial writing, you are just asking friends for response and input.

Sometimes, we might feel like we are "bothering" colleagues when we ask for their input. Here are a few things to keep in mind. Be sure to give responders a good amount of time to make space in their schedule. That gives you time to set aside the project and clear your head. How long to give them? That's hard to say. I would suggest six to ten weeks for reading a book. Shorter for an article or essay (four to six weeks?). Second, let responders know what kind of feedback you want and how much. For some, it might be too much work to give extensive comments. They might want to just give general feedback. For others, they enjoy reading and providing more detailed notes. Third, offer to read *their* work and give comments. Think of it as a feedback *community*, where there is give and take. Finally, while it is helpful to have all kinds of people give feedback (like fellow professors or doctoral students), I find it appropriate to seek out people who fit the "target audience." Some of my books and articles are geared towards pastors (not academic researchers). I might have a fellow academic read the work to catch specific mistakes in scholarship, but I also want a pastor or two to give it a read to make sure it reaches the main audience.

So after you get the feedback—then what? If there are corrections to typos and grammar, I go through and make those changes. Usually the responder is catching something I missed. When it comes to comments regarding content and argumentation, I try to collect all those notes from responders and spend time thinking about whether or not those comments will improve the work. Usually, I try to address the majority of concerns from responders. Sometimes that requires a clarifying sentence or paragraph; at other times it might necessitate adding a whole section or chapter. Take your time, plan carefully and thoughtfully, and follow your instincts. Again, in most circumstances your publishing editor will be there at the next stage to help refine your work.

From Writing to Publication

In this chapter, we have looked at the writing process. Everyone writes in their own way, but there are some best practices and formative habits. We have talked about some of my approaches and habits that I have picked up along the way. In the next chapter we will move from writing to publishing. Research and writing are the most laborious parts of the process. But the book, essay, or article only becomes a product for public consumption when it is published. We will address the reasons for and nature of publishing, and the process of working with publishers.

5

Getting Your Work Published

WHEN IT COMES TO being a writer, the product matters. The product needs to be worthwhile. But the reality is, it also matters that the product gets to the target audience. This is where publishers come in. They play the role of helping to make the textual product the best it can be, and they take on the responsibility of selling and promoting the work. And it really *matters* that writers find the right publisher for their work. It pays to do your due diligence to make sure you found the right fit in a publisher.

When I was a doctoral student, a group of us were walking around the book stalls at the annual meeting of the Society of Biblical Literature. We were like kids in a candy shop—dozens of publishers had booths set up with their latest book wares. At one small table there was a man who apparently was the head of an academic press. He called out to us as we were walking by, "Are you PhD students?" We nodded affirmatively. He followed up, "Hey, if you sign here that you will publish your dissertation with me after you pass your defense, I will give a contract to you right now." We looked at each other in disbelief. *This guy wants to give us contracts before we even finish?* Needless to say, we slowly backed away, never to return. Let this be a cautionary tale that some publishers have low standards, and with that comes a not-so-great reputation. You want to publish your work with reputable publishers who do high quality production, have experienced editors, and are known for making important contributions to the field.

Every now and again, I hear chatter online about the benefits of "self-publishing." *Cut out the middleman!*, they say. *Why give a cut of my profits to the publisher, when I can put the book out myself?* I can see the attraction, because easier and cheaper can sometimes seem worth it. There are new digital tools that make it possible to produce a book all by yourself with a few clicks. But I want to convince you that working with a reputable publisher is worth the time, effort, and cost. At the very least, publishers offer their expertise in sharpening your work. Publishers with a strong reputation have a devoted following, people *trust* them and pay attention to their work.

For beginner writers, the world of publishing can be a mystery. So, let's start with the "who" questions: who are the people behind the publishing companies?

President/Publisher. This is the highest level admin (though there may be a separate owner). Authors don't interface directly with the president, but they may sign off on contracts.

Acquisitions editor. This person is the main contact for authors who are shopping around their book idea or manuscript. More on that later.

Project editor/copyeditor. Once a book proposal has been accepted and a contract is issued, the editors are the professionals who help authors get the work completed towards a final manuscript. They assist in managing the manuscript through to the end, sometimes they act as the technical copyeditor as well.

Series editor. Sometimes a book may belong to a series, and the series editor will play a role in acquiring books and in giving feedback on the manuscript. In many cases, the series editor does not "work" for the publisher. They are academics (in most cases with jobs at colleges or universities) who also edit a series. They may get paid (usually a percentage of the royalties), or they may not.

Marketing professional. You may work with someone in marketing to make a plan for helping to promote and sell the book. If you are working with a more "academic" publisher (that doesn't sell trade books), there is less of a chance that you will get intentional and extensive marketing support.

Let's get into one of the most common questions that authors ask: *How do I choose a publisher?* In biblical studies, for example, there are dozens of publishers. There are university presses, evangelical publishers, denominational publishers, ones that focus on world religions (of which Christianity and Judaism are two areas), and more besides. Perhaps, the first thing to do is have a clear sense of the topic and audience of your book idea. Then, you can try to match that up with a publisher that has a track record of producing high quality books in that field. In the world of biblical studies, there is also something to say about where the book topic falls on the spectrum of theological or ideological commitments. And some publishers want to try to reach a very large audience (perhaps of pastors, students, and laypeople), and maybe others tend to concentrate on very specific groups ("scholars only").

One way to process the "choosing a publisher" issue is to think through: *who are the dialogue partners in my topic and the wider conversation?* Maybe you can come up with ten to twenty scholars who write articles and books on similar subjects. *Where do they publish their work? For which publishers do they tend to write endorsements?* A further step would be to reach out to some of those colleagues and ask about their experiences, why they chose the publishers they did, and if they recommend them to you.[1]

How Do You Make Contact With a Publisher?

I'll tell you what you don't do. You don't send a random email to an editor you don't know, or to a generic email address like info@publisher.org. Cold contact is not a successful strategy for getting your academic book contracted or published. In many cases, a personal connection is the way to go. There are two common ways that authors connect to acquisitions editors. First, you have opportunities that arise at academic conferences (like AAR/SBL). Editors often plan their lives around the major conferences and see important opportunities to meet up with friends and colleagues, old and new. You could just walk up to the exhibition booth for a publisher and hope to get a chance to meet with an editor. But, the reality is that many editors fill up their schedules ahead of time to make sure they see certain authors and manage their time well. So, I wouldn't count on editors being available on the spot. The best bet is to email an editor ahead of time, maybe a month or so before a conference, and ask politely for a chance to visit and connect to talk about a book project.

---

1. In Appendix A, I walk through my publishing journey, so you might want to skip ahead and read that to get a sense for why I worked with the people that I did, and how some of my opportunities came to be.

That brings me to the *second* way to connect with a publisher. *"Phone-a-friend."* As in, ask a more senior colleague (or doctoral supervisor, for example) to make an email introduction for you. This can warm an editor over to meeting you. Editors are busy—yes, they want to meet up-and-coming scholars, but a recommendation from a respected scholar whom they already know can go a long way. Keep contact emails with editors professional, polite, short, and to the point. *Do not send them long emails.* They will loathe it. And don't send editors a whole book document on first contact. There are some preliminary things that work best before you get to the stage of sending the whole thing to a publisher.

So, let's say you are lucky enough to have an opportunity to present your book idea to an editor—hurray! Now you need to plan out and practice your book pitch.

The Book Pitch

Maybe your book pitch opportunity is in person, maybe it is over Zoom, maybe it is via email. It all works about the same, but personally I like the in-person, because the editor gets a better feel for your personality and the potential working relationship. But what exactly is entailed in a pitch? The goal is to grab the attention and interest of the editor. You want to convince them that your book idea is (1) a good fit for their specific "brand" or type of books and (2) relatively novel. And (3) you will need to present yourself as the right person to write that book. Now, many of these editors are experienced in the book business, so it won't pay to *oversell* the idea or yourself ("Everyone will want to read this book!")—that approach often comes across as either naive or arrogant. On the other hand, you don't want to undersell yourself either ("It's not a great idea, but it's all I've got"). There is a happy medium of quiet confidence and optimism, drawing from expertise, that focuses on great ideas, not self-promotion.

You might be having a long lunch with an editor at a conference, a short coffee sit-down, or sometimes just a hallway chat in passing. In any case, a good book pitch can be short and to the point (leaving the editor interested and wanting to hear more). *I have this idea for a book. The big research question is [X]. To be honest, I am surprised there aren't a lot of other books on this subject. (Or, other books on this subject always seem to miss [Y].) The angle I want to take is [Z]. Here are some (quick) contributions I think I can make on this issue. My experience and expertise involve [A, B, C].*

Don't use this as a script, but you get the idea. If this is your first or second pitch, you might want to practice a two-to-three minute "elevator" book pitch. Experienced editors will have a good general knowledge of biblical scholarship, enough to know if you really know what you are talking about. It will definitely be worth your while to know as much as you can about the publisher, what kinds of topics and methods are commonly found in their recent catalog of books, and what theological and ideological commitments they have. Then you can be clear and direct about how your idea might be a fit for them.

What happens next? For new authors, editors tend not to make any commitment on the spot. Most likely, if the editor is interested, they will follow up and ask for an official proposal, sometimes a writing sample. You might leave the first meeting with a good vibe, or the editor may hold their cards close. Or, unfortunately, you might get the impression that you will never hear from them again. Keep in mind, acquisitions editors have a lot of influence in turning a good book proposal into an official contract, but usually they have to present the book to a publishing board that makes the final decision. In that sense, if the acquisitions editor really likes your book idea, they act as a kind of agent or advocate when they go into the "pub board" meeting. The bottom line is this: if you impress the acquisitions editor, this is only a first (albeit crucial) step in moving towards an official contract. If all goes well, the next step is writing up an official book proposal.

Writing Up a Book Proposal

I recall how intimidated I was when I first tried to write up a book proposal. I wasn't sure exactly what kind of information to provide, or how much. There is no rulebook for length, tone, and style. Like many things, it is often a matter of learning by experience, a bit of trial and error, and old fashioned luck. But there are some standard or common features of academic book proposals that we can talk about.

Book Title/Subtitle: I suggest keeping your proposed book title information clear and straightforward. Academic books don't tend to have artsy or mysterious titles. If you *do* want to consider a clever title, that can be negotiated later. Publishers spend a lot of time thinking through titling and how to make sure the book gets to the right audience through SEO (Search Engine Optimization) keywords. At this stage of the proposal, the purpose of listing the title is to help the editors and other pub board members (like sales and marketing) get a quick, "at-a-glance" sense of the subject matter.

Book Description: It is not advisable to write a lengthy book description in the proposal. Some of the "big ideas" of the book can be offered in the table of contents section (see below). Here, the goal is to present the need for the book and the basic content in such a way that the pub board thinks "we have to have this book, it fits who we are, it is fresh and interesting." How long should a book description be? My tendency is to offer about a page worth of information (200–300 words).

Audience: Who would the book be written for? This is a matter of knowing your readership, pitching the book to the right level. Don't just say "everyone!" A book written for everyone might end up being read by no one. Imagine what kind of person is going to buy your book. Actually try to think of specific people in your head. Do you picture a student? What level? Undergraduate freshman stepping into a Bible course for the first time? Or a senior who has a good amount of background knowledge? Or a graduate student? Or maybe a fellow scholar, who would not be intimidated by the use of Aramaic or Coptic?

Now, you actually might have different kinds of readers in mind, some books do fit that dynamic. In those cases, I tend to think in terms of concentric circles. The "bullseye" is the "perfect audience," the specific reader that you wrote the book for. But then, one circle out, you may have in mind a broader group that might still be interested. For example, I wrote an introduction to Philippians in a book series that caters to students (*Reading Philippians* in Cascade's "Companions" series). But I thought that it could also serve as a kind of Bible study for church groups. So, you could mention a "primary audience" and a "secondary audience."

Comparable Books: Publishers want to know that authors are offering something interesting and "new" to the field. If you say, "I want to write a New Testament Greek textbook," the natural question is: with dozens of Greek textbooks already published, why would someone use yours instead? It's an important question, because publishers want to sell books that make a difference, and authors want to write books that meet some intellectual need.

When publishers ask about comparable books that are already in existence, they want to know if there is market space for another book on the subject. Keep in mind, this is always an open question, and there is room to make your case that you bring something original and fresh to the wider discussion. Let's revisit the Greek textbook idea. Yes, there are lots of Greek textbooks that are already in circulation. But maybe what you bring is a new method or approach. Or maybe it is about the types of exercises and workbook features you have in mind. When you list comparable books and resources, try to be honest (don't hide anything), and also explain clearly and directly how your own book idea compares and differs.

Table of Contents with Brief Descriptions: This is the chance to walk the pub board through the book in more detail. I think of this as a kind of "storyboarding" of the book idea: it's in short and somewhat raw form, but it gives them a sense of how the book will flow from beginning to end, from research questions through ideas and arguments to some kind of answer or response.

Total Word Count: A brief and straightforward answer here is sufficient. Publishers want to know what kind of investment is involved in this project, whether the word count fits the type of book, and how best it works for the audience. If you haven't written any chapters of the book ahead of time, the total word count tends to be a guess, and publishers know that. It is obviously helpful to make a *good* guess (that gets close to what the final word count will be), but they don't expect authors to limit themselves rigidly to a specific number. They want a reasonable ballpark figure. *Is this a 50,000 word (short) book? A 100,000 word (medium size) book? Or a 200,000 word (large) book?* You might look at comparable books on the subject and make a guess as to whether you want to write more, less, or about the same amount. That will help you determine a target word count.

Delivery Date: Obviously, the publisher wants to know the timeline—when will you complete the full manuscript? As with word count, there is a bit of flexibility here. But keep in mind publishers plan out their lineup of new books year by year, thinking through workload, staffing, best times of year to release books, etc. You want to be realistic about when you can reasonably complete the manuscript. This is usually not a deal-breaker issue for a publisher, but more a factor that helps with planning.

Author Expertise: Publishers want "good idea" books, obviously, and they also want authors of excellence. It's one thing to have an idea, it's another thing to be able to follow through with a great complete manuscript. How do you prove expertise? Sometimes the publisher wants an up-to-date CV, where they can see your educational background, research or teaching context, previous publications, and experience and involvement in the guild. More specifically, they want to know that you have worked or published in the same general area. If you are new to book publishing, they might ask for a letter of recommendation from a doctoral supervisor.

This should go without saying, but make sure that your CV only contains information that is directly pertinent to supporting the case for getting a contract for the book. So, for example, you don't need to include your pet names, or that you play the banjo well and won a local pie-eating contest. (Unless the book is about banjos and pies.)

Writing Sample. Sometimes, the publisher may want to read a sample chapter *before* they issue an official contract. This tends to be the case when an academic press is working with a scholar new to book publishing. The chapter should represent well the tone, expertise, and subject matter of the book.

A word to the wise: a book proposal is a crucial "first impression" when connecting with a publisher for the first time in writing. So, it is important that you make sure the proposal is very well written and completely free of typos and spelling mistakes. It is well worth your while to make the proposal as neat and clean as you can. Getting some feedback from experienced peers and mentors on a book proposal can be helpful.

Outcomes. It could take weeks, sometimes months, for an acquisitions editor to get back to you with a verdict from the pub board, so be patient. The happiest scenario is an email that starts like this: "Good news, your proposal was accepted." But it could also go the other way ("While we liked some of the ideas in this proposal, it's just not a great fit for us at this time..."). Or, it is often the case in my experience that the pub board asks for some adjustments and revisions to the proposal, or more information. The acquisitions editor acts as a kind of go-between to help you nuance and re-shape to fulfill the needs and desires of both the author and publisher.

Contracts and Expectations

Let's say you worked it out and won over the pub board—now it is time to work on a contract. Here are the basics: a contract sets the terms of business that safeguards both the author and the publisher. Book contracts can be long with lots of fine print, but here are the key items.

Book details. The contract will reflect many of the details already discussed in the accepted proposal: title, subject/description, length, delivery date. The author is responsible for sticking close to these commitments (within reason).

Payment/royalties and benefits. The contract lays out clearly how the author will be compensated. From my experience, academic authors receive between six to fifteen percent royalties on book sales, depending on the publisher's preferences and the author's potential for high sales.[2] If you are a new author in the arena of publishing, you don't really have much bargaining power. My advice: take what is offered. Once you have published a few books (and sales have gone reasonably well), then you have more experience and knowledge on your side, and it becomes more appropriate to bargain.

Sometimes the publisher will offer an advance (on royalties).[3] You're not Stephen King or J. K. Rowling, so we're not talking ten million dollars. For academic books, generally speaking, getting an advance at all is a rare gift. But if one is offered, it is in the hundreds of dollars for us mere mortals. It is a privilege for an author to receive an advance, because it is a vote of confidence on the part of the publisher. Publishers are risk-averse, so they are taking a chance on an author by offering money up front. If the book did not hit the sales targets they projected, they might be looking at a loss. That's not the author's fault per se, and the publisher would not blame an author for poor sales (except in the case of a legal issue or moral failure that harmed the reputation of the author, book, or publisher). But it is helpful to know that with an advance issued, the publisher has bet on the success of the book—that's a good thing, and will mean they are committed to doing everything in their power to get it into the hands of readers.

What other benefits might be offered in a contract? The publisher usually outlines the number of free author copies (around five to ten), special

---

2. I have signed a couple of contracts where I have received *no* royalties. These tend to be publishers that only produce advanced academic monographs where there is not much financial profit expected.

3. Sometimes an advance is paid to the author in full immediately after the contract is signed. Sometimes an advance is paid when the book manuscript is submitted and deemed acceptable. And sometimes the advance is split, partially paid after the contract is signed, and then the remainder given after the manuscript is complete.

author discounts on their own books, and possibly other related deals like royalties from audio book versions, foreign translations, etc. New authors tend to take whatever the publisher offers, and in my experience most publishers follow an industry standard.

Legal matters. Contracts contain lots of legal information that should be read carefully. For obvious reasons, publishers would hold the author liable for issues of plagiarism, breach of contract, and any way that the author has not delivered on what was promised. All things being equal, publishers are not greedy or petty. They don't terminate contracts flippantly. The acquisitions editor plays a mediating and relationship-building role, so there ought to be a lot of good will on both sides.

My advice for new authors at the contracting stage is to trust your acquisitions editor. You are forging a new relationship with a publisher, and trust is really important. Take what they offer and see how the publishing experience goes. If a new author is really pushy, or asks for too much, it can come across as arrogant or naive, in either case that could be a red flag for a publisher.

Canceling a Contract?

What if you want to cancel a contract after the fact? Can this be done? How easy is it? What are the risks? These are important questions, and a lot depends on the situation and the reasons for termination. Canceling a contract is not particularly hard or impossible, but in many cases it does weaken your relationship with the editor and publisher, so it is never something that should be done lightly. Let's say it is for health reasons, or loss of job. I am sure your editor would be sympathetic. They might offer an extension, allowing you more time to complete the manuscript. Life happens, publishers know that. When COVID hit, like everyone else, my life got turned upside down. I reached out to a few publishers I was working with and requested extensions on contracts, in some cases asking for more than a year's delay—they were all flexible and understanding. I didn't ask to cancel any contracts, but if I did, I think my editors would have encouraged me to take an extra year or two to get my situation settled, and then see what happens (rather than issue a termination immediately). My point, though, is that publishers know that life can get messy and things change, and they plan and assume some flexibility when it comes to contracts and deadlines.

Now let's say you sign the dotted line with a book contract with Publisher A, and then Publisher B comes along and wants that same book and gives you more attractive benefits. Can you break off with A and sign up with B? The short answer is: no. This obviously would hurt your relationship with A, and it is considered unprofessional. The long answer is: check the fine print of your contract. Often, book contracts explain that you are committing your book idea to the publisher you sign a contract with. If you cancel that contract, you can't take that book idea somewhere else. Let's say you are not having a positive experience with Publisher A, and that is the reason you want to terminate the contract. I suggest having an open and honest conversation with your editor and try to work things out. Again, by and large, editors care about the working relationships they have with authors and want to do as much as they can to ensure that authors feel heard, valued, and supported.

Do I Need A Literary Agent?

The short answer is: no. You might think to yourself, *am I getting the best contract deal? How do I get access to big name publishers?* But if you are writing in an academic (or semi-academic) context, most authors don't have agents. If you get to the place in your career where you are negotiating a five-figure advance, or you expect to sell 10,000 copies or more of your latest book, then it might be time to consider an agent. But for the rest of us, we continue to work directly with editors and negotiate our own contracts. Now, it does pay to talk through contract items with trusted mentors and colleagues who have a bit more experience. The more you know, the further you'll go.

Publishing with Magazines

Before moving on, I want to briefly address my experience with magazine writing.[4] It is not a general expectation that academics write for more popular level publications like newspapers (op-ed) or magazines. And, yet,

---

4. I have written for *Christianity Today, Christian Century, Bible Study Magazine,* and *Fathom Magazine.*

sometimes theologians and Bible scholars wind up doing some of this kind of writing. Personally, I enjoy it, because I remember how much I benefited from reading Christian magazines in my student years, and I still benefit from a good magazine article today. It is a special service that an academic can provide to the wider world, lending their expertise on a biblical, theological, cultural, moral, or philosophical question. So how do you actually get an opportunity to write for a magazine?

I'll tell you (again) how you *don't do it*! A handful of years ago, I had an idea for a magazine article. I wrote up the article and then I uploaded it to a magazine's webpage where you can submit unsolicited work. A few weeks later, I received a polite, but clearly automated, response that they decided not to publish the article. (Surprise, surprise.) I am sure they get dozens of pitches each week from strangers, so they reject a lot of stuff.

There is a better way to get on a magazine's radar, I think, and it doesn't take a genius to figure it out (especially given some of the "secrets" I have mentioned in this chapter): you gotta *know* someone that *knows* someone at the magazine. So, I asked a friend I know who writes for the magazine to (email) introduce me to an editor. And they did. Then I was able to make a pitch, and the rest, as they say, is history.

But before you ask that friend for a favor, there are some things you need to know about working with a magazine. First, they are not looking only or primarily for eggheads, people that are super intelligent and know lots of stuff. Those kinds of people don't always make great magazine writers. They are looking for people who know what they are talking about who are also great writers that can connect with a broad audience of non-experts. There's a certain rhetorical skill involved, and good magazine editors can sniff it out. So, if you happen to make contact with a real, live magazine editor, they are going to want to know if you can write well to their readership. And, I pretty much guarantee they are going to "Google" you. They want to find writing that you have done that is comparable to magazine level (blogs? Maybe podcast interviews? Youtube videos?). And they probably want to know what kind of online presence you have, how you engage with people online, and whether or not you might be a liability in any way. All of that to say, magazine editors choose their writers very carefully, so be prepared to be vetted. It's not a bad thing, it's just a part of the process.

If you really want to write a magazine article or two, my advice is this: connect with an editor and pitch them an idea or two. Sometimes you hit it off, and sometimes you don't. They might take one idea, and not the next. I have only written a handful of magazine articles, but my habit is to shop around an idea. You look for who is the best fit for the article idea, and hopefully a magazine has interest, time, and space to make it a reality.

In this chapter, we introduced the publishing world and how to connect with acquisitions editors. We also addressed basics of book proposals and publishing contracts. In the next chapter, we will return to the world of book publishing. After you submit your book manuscript to the editor, the next stage of the book's pre-public life begins.

6

Editing and Final Publication Processes

IT IS A GREAT feeling when an author finishes writing a manuscript and presses "send" on the email to the editor. Take a nap. Treat yourself to a nice meal. Go on that tropical vacation. But . . . that is not the end of the process. It is a major stage on the journey, but there is still more work to be done to get the book ready for its world debut. In this chapter we will talk about what it is like to move through editorial steps with the publisher, and then finalize the process, culminating in that beautiful box that arrives on your doorstep with *gratis* author copies.

Publisher's Review of Manuscript and Author Revision. When you send your completed manuscript to the publisher, specifically to your editor, this initiates a chain of events that move your book towards final publication. Your editor, or perhaps another one (depending on the publisher's workflow systems), works through your document and gives feedback and corrections. Sometimes the publisher will send the document to an external reviewer (an academic with expertise in your subject area) for feedback. All of this will be communicated to the author.

Part of the review process is making sure that the manuscript conforms to "house style," the academic style used by the publisher. Usually, at the contracting stage, the author is given the house style. Sometimes these documents can be tediously long; of course, you should look through them, but I often find it more helpful to look at recent books from the publisher to study examples of their house style (especially footnote citation style).

What kind of feedback is given to authors? It can be all sorts of things, on the whole-book level (*you might add a short chapter on [XYZ]?*), to section comments (*this anecdote/illustration is not helpful*), to granular details (*you might consider citing [so-and-so] here*). Some publishers and editors give lots of comments, feedback, and corrections; others give hardly any, and are just looking to tidy up the manuscript. Whatever the case, you are meant to go through the document and interact with their corrections and answer their questions. They will usually give you a deadline of several weeks in order to keep the publication schedule on track.

Can authors say "no" to requested changes? That's a fair question and there is a bit of negotiation that can happen at this stage. On the one hand, it is inadvisable to be completely stubborn and refuse most or all correction requests. The book is a project that brings together the knowledge and wisdom of the author with the experience and resources of the publisher—there is an expectation of these two parties uniting to make the book the best that it can be. But, on the other hand, the author's name is on the cover, in a sense it is *their* book, so the author has a right to push back if they feel like a certain change is a problem. My tendency is to accept most or all of the minor changes, and then to have a big think about the major ones. Editors, by and large, are used to working with academic authors and expect there will be give-and-take when it comes to major changes. So, if a requested major change rubs you the wrong way, have a conversation with your editor. It's perfectly fine to say, "Hey, you recommended taking out this section, I really like it and want to keep it, can we talk more about other options, like revision or putting it in an appendix?" Or, "You suggested cutting the conclusion in half, what if I can shave it down by a quarter? I really like the material there."

There might be a bit of a back-and-forth that happens with queries, edits, more suggestions, and so forth. Editors are busy, they are usually working on multiple projects at once or have a queue of other projects waiting for them, so they are not motivated to let a revision process drag on slowly. Eventually, the manuscript editing is complete, author and editor are happy (hopefully!), and then the book moves on to the "page proofs" stage. *How much time does it take to do revisions?* There is no magic formula, because each book is different and each person is different. For some of my shorter and more basic books, revisions sometimes only took a few hours (mostly cleaning up typos and adding a few clarifying statements).

Editing and Final Publication Processes

For bigger projects, I have dedicated twenty to thirty hours to careful revision and can involve adding a new section.

Proofs Stage. What are "page proofs"? These pages comprise the final version of the manuscript that is meant to look like the actual book (headings, columns, margins, spacing, etc.). Normally, authors are given a chance to read through the proofs and identify any mistakes or recommend minor changes. This is a crucial step, because it is the last chance to catch typos and errors. There is an old adage, "You will not find any typos at the proofs stage, but when the book is published and you crack open your own book for the first time—you will immediately spot *all* of them and die of embarrassment." (Also known as Murphy's Law.) The temptation for some authors (like me) is to rush through proofs, anxious to get the process done with and see the book in print. But we need to resist those urges and do the patient, hard work of slow and careful proofreading.

My habit is to print out the manuscript—even if it is a few hundred pages. And then I sit in a comfortable chair with a red pen and go through the document page by page. What am I looking for? Obviously, I want to catch spelling errors and wrong wording. But also I glance at Scripture references (you don't want any "2 Corinthians 14" or "Psalm 166"). And I double check Greek and Hebrew text, to make sure nothing strange happened with letter order (Hebrew) or accents (Greek).

Your editor or someone else at the publisher will let you know how to provide corrections and changes. Back in the old days, you might have to mail a stack of papers with handwritten corrections. But in the digital age, corrections can be done through an emailed annotated PDF or "track changes" Word document.

Once the editor has made the changes and approved edits, they will create a new set of proofs. Sometimes they will send "second proofs" to the author for their approval. If the process is running according to plan, that is the end of the proofing process. If the author spots more problems, then there might be another back-and-forth.

Usually the last step in the manuscript finalization process is every author's least favorite part of writing and publishing: *indexing.*

Indexing. Academic books tend to have indexes. We use them, we value them, we need them. *We also hate to produce them.* And yet, someone has to do that tedious work, and at least in the academy the convention is that that burden falls to the author. Often the author and editor come to some agreement as to what kinds of indexes are necessary for the book. (Modern author? Ancient texts? Subject index?) Whatever is finally decided, the procedure is pretty straightforward. The publisher sends the author a final (or nearly final) version of the book, and a set of instructions for how to format the index.

A few years ago, a friend who was new to publishing asked me about the least tedious method of producing the index. Sadly, there is no secret shortcut; we all pretty much do the same thing: work page-by-page through the manuscript and write down the indexed items on a separate document. It is boring and tiresome, but there is really no way around it. The good news is that once you get to the indexing stage, the book is nearly done—that is something to be excited about!

Now, a lucky few authors can afford to pay for their book to be indexed by someone else. There are a couple of options here. Most publishers offer a paid service where they contract a professional to create the indexes. These publisher-contracted indexers are very thorough and accurate, but also very expensive. You might have to pay $500–$1500 for an index.

Another option is to pay a student or friend to create the indexes. This is a pretty common practice, because (one's own) students might be eager to be involved in a book project, and would be willing to take less money (I generally pay about $300 as an "indexing stipend," sometimes out of my own pocket). Occasionally, I index the book myself (if I imagine it will be relatively short and easy).[1] I have been told before—and I believe it is true based on my own experience—the author is best suited to create the indexes, because they know the subject matter the best. One major benefit of the author doing this work is that it provides *one last* reading of the book page-by-page. Truth be told (don't tell anyone I told you this), I have found several of my own typos at the indexing stage.

The publisher will usually give you an optimal timeline for completing the indexes in order to keep the book on schedule for release.

Front matter, back cover. At some point after completing the manuscript, you will need to work on the book's "Front matter." This is a generic way of

---

1. You might wonder—*isn't there some kind of software that can "auto-generate" indexes?* Things like that do exist, but very few academic publishers use them. Part of the problem is the highly technical nature of academic books. Computer programs would have a hard time processing the right material and building indexes accurately and comprehensively. Thus, even if a program made a "first pass" at indexing, someone would need to double-check everything anyway.

talking about some of the material at the beginning of the book, such as abbreviation list, acknowledgments and preface, official table of contents, and dedication page. Writing acknowledgments offers a special opportunity to recognize colleagues and friends who have helped shape you and your work. A preface, not always included or needed, sets up the background and context for the book from a personal or professional standpoint. A short dedication puts a personal touch on the book.

I don't need to explain to you what a Table of Contents (TOC) is, but one thing to consider is how detailed the TOC should be. Sometimes, I encounter TOCs that are frustratingly short—just a few short (sometimes cryptic) chapter titles. Alternatively, I have seen TOCs that are absurdly long, listing out not just sections and chapters, but all the subsection headings. That might be helpful for a textbook, but for most other books it is overkill and ends up not helping readers find the information they are looking for quickly and easily. All things being equal, I prefer more detailed TOCs, for the simple reason that readers will often turn to the TOC (on the publisher's website, GoogleBooks, or Amazon) to get a sense for the subjects covered in the book. A vague, cryptic, or frustratingly brief TOC could turn off potential readers.

Sometimes, the publisher will ask the author for a book description and some language to use on the back cover. Other times, they have their own people come up with that material (which might fall more into the territory of marketing and promotion). It's hard to overestimate the importance of the back cover description. That is often the paragraph used in marketing and found on bookseller websites. When potential readers come across your book, aside from the cover, the back cover description is often the main piece of information they read about your work.

Endorsers. Publishers might also request a possible list of endorsers, colleagues, and recognized experts who can vouch for the quality of the book, its ideas, and expression. Usually, they ask the author for a list of suggested endorsers whom they can approach. There is ongoing academic discussion about the benefit of back cover and inside-jacket endorsements. The content of the endorsements, i.e., the actual comments, don't tend to matter much. Rarely is something of substance said that is not communicated by the book description itself. What appears to make more of a difference is *who* the endorsers are, namely trusted voices that may draw attention to the book. It is kind of like "If you like this music, you might also like . . . "

websites. It places the book in conversation with certain scholars who are known and respected in the same area.

Foreword? A "foreword" is a short essay or statement made in the front matter by a *different* author (usually of more senior status) that draws out the significance of the contribution of the book. The name of the foreword author usually goes on the book cover as a special feature that helps bring extra attention, and perhaps a bit of *gravitas*, to the book.

Cover Design. I love books (that should be obvious by now). I love the smell of books, the textures, attractive fonts, and different binding types. But one of my favorite things is appreciating a good book cover. Some publishers go with more classic and plain cover styles, some put a lot of work into artistic designs. I like them both. *What input do authors have in cover design?* It depends on the publisher and perhaps also on the series. Some publishers and series have a set design. For other publishers, they create an individual design for each book. If you happen to be working with the latter, it is often the case that authors are consulted in some fashion. Some publishers will send authors a set of questions about colors, designs, and images that come to mind when they think about the book. From there, the publisher's graphic designer produces a cover. In other situations, the designer might send the editor and author a few options and they can discuss and choose. I have seen a situation or two where the author has a very specific idea for the cover (like a particular piece of art), and that is used. If you know the publisher creates unique covers for their books (or specifically in the series in which your book appears), there is no harm in asking to have some input. Publishers want their authors to be satisfied with all design aspects of the book (within reason). There is an unspoken expectation that goes along with that—it is impolite and even disrespectful for an author to complain publicly about the design of their published book. Better to have these conversations with the publisher before publication when adjustments and changes can be made.

Pricing?

Does the author have a say in the book's pricing? The short answer is no. Publishers have their own systems for deciding pricing and authors have no say, and there really isn't an opportunity to give input. Now, where there *might* be some leverage is whether your book is a (more expensive) hardcover or a (less expensive) softcover. You might think, "cheap is always better." But publishers are risk-averse and authors can usually expect that they will know best the binding/cost situation that best suits the book and maximizes sales potential. The bottom line is that an early career/novice writer should not get involved in the pricing conversation. For more experienced writers, I might suggest asking at the contracting stage about binding type and cost range. There might be a possibility for some wiggle room or negotiation.

In this chapter, we have described and discussed the work involved in a book *after* the submission of the manuscript and *before* publication. There is actually quite a lot to do at this stage, and these activities are important for the excellence and success of the published book. Once all of this is complete, the book is finalized on the publisher's end and sent into printing. It might seem like a book about writing and publishing would end there—*tada! The book is done!* But actually, the preparatory work is finished, the book gets printed and bound, but there are still some things to think about and do. The author can contribute to helping the book thrive in its new life in the world.

7

After the Book Is Published

THERE IS A NICE moment when you can check off the following boxes:

- ~~I turned in the manuscript to the editor~~
- ~~I responded to feedback from the editor~~
- ~~I checked first page proofs~~
- ~~I wrote acknowledgments and dedication~~
- ~~I checked second proofs~~
- ~~I wrote the index (darn indexing!)~~
- ~~I read through the whole thing one more time~~
- ~~I got the email from the publisher that the book is off to the printer.~~

It might seem like the work is done, but there are some things you can do to help your book get some attention and interest from the target audiences. So, don't move on to the next book just yet. The *pre-work* for the book's life is complete and that is worth celebrating. But now it must be born and live life out there in the world with other people. And you have more to do!

Like what? Promoting the book, discussing the book, and responding to engagement in whatever ways you can and want to. I always find it sad when an author puts dozens or hundreds of hours into publishing a book and then moves on to the next project without much thought about the "life" of the work. But if you want to help insure that your book actually generates a conversation, you need to have a long-term plan for increasing

After the Book Is Published

the exposure and volume of that work. Now, some writers balk at the idea of promoting their own book. As if it is arrogant and self-serving. But remember, when you first conceived of writing that book, what drove you was the desire for that idea to get out there, to change the world (or one small corner of the world), to inspire a fresh conversation. And that should continue to motivate you to promote your ideas after the book is actually out! Of course, there are good ways to promote your work, and bad ways to do it. A bad way would be to overwhelm social media with rhapsodic tweets about how amazing your book is. It's also not a good idea to "oversell" the work: "*No book like this has ever been published!*" "*Groundbreaking!*" "*An instant bestseller!*" You don't want someone to pick up your work and be disappointed that it didn't live up to the hype. Better to focus on what you *do* offer.

So, what are tried and true ways of promoting one's own work? First, academic book reviews have been the traditional way of getting your book some traction in the wider guild. Many publishers are more than willing to send a copy or two to journals. It is worth considering which journals with review sections are the biggest bang for your buck, so to speak. For traditional academic books, *Review of Biblical Literature*, *The Catholic Biblical Quarterly*, *Journal of Theological Studies*, and *Bulletin for Biblical Research* are widely read with longer book reviews. Academic reviews won't give your book wide exposure, but positive academic reviews in respected journals are coveted. Another way to draw interest to your academic book is to see if a conference session might organize a book review panel (e.g., at Society of Biblical Literature). The challenge with that approach is that conference program units often plan their annual sessions far in advance, but it is worth a try. Other ways to attract interest in your book include sending book information to some of the clubs or societies that you are a part of. It might be a denominational club, a theological society, or a topical group (like archaeology or Second Temple Judaism studies). Sometimes, publishers will do a promotional book giveaway over social media.

If you have a blog or website, you might consider talking about your work and the contributions you are trying to make for the academy or society. Or, consider contacting a magazine or society website to share one of your key ideas in short form. Right now (2022), podcasts are all the rage. If you (or the publisher) happen to have connections to academic-oriented podcasts, you might seek out an interview opportunity. Obviously, thousands of books are published every year, so these kinds of high-exposure opportunities are very limited.

Keep in mind, the publisher might have their own plan for promotion and advertisement. Some publishers do a lot of ads, some do a little, and some do none. For those that have a more robust budget and plan for promotion, they might invest in social media ads, journal ads, email blasts, ads in society newsletters, video interviews, etc. But publishers appreciate when the author takes time to engage with their own networks about their latest work.

Now, there is a line that an author can cross where it seems like too much self-promotion. Sometimes it is hard to discern where exactly that line is, but I have heard an 80/20 principle: an author should focus on their own work on social media (or their own blog) only 20 percent of the time, the rest should concentrate on the work of others. One way, then, to pique interest in your own new work may be to talk about influences on your ideas (in the works of others). These would function as reading recommendations. It takes some creativity to generate a conversation for the book; consult with your publisher to coordinate efforts.

One last thing to consider in the early life of the book: online reviews make a difference. It is worth encouraging friends and students to leave a legitimate review on their favorite store or reading websites like Amazon or GoodReads. These are places where readers go to see quick takes on new (and old) books. Amazon reviews are not always fair or accurate, obviously. No one is fact-checking reviews. So, a single review, or a set of trolling reviews, don't always tell you the value of a book. Correspondingly, a string of good reviews also doesn't mean a book is "right." But when a book gets a significant number of reviews (let's say 50+), and many of them are positive, it raises the profile of the book. That can be advantageous for getting the book on the radar of the target audience.

Sometimes I sense from authors that they don't feel it is their job to promote their own work, that should be a burden carried by the publisher. But publishers often respond that authors miss out on introducing their own book to their community, when they have this attitude. If you are completely at a loss for how to promote your work, have a chat with your publisher, especially the marketing, promotion, and sales reps. They can give you some ideas based on what has worked in the past for them. My take is this: doing something as an author usually helps, doing nothing does nothing. As an author, you spend hundreds of hours dreaming, researching, writing, editing, rewriting, and finishing up the project. Why not do what you can to introduce your work to interested communities and readers?

Reviews of Your Book: The Good, the Bad, and the Ugly

Authors *want* their books reviewed. It is an honor to have a colleague read your work and take it seriously enough to write up a professional review. But I always cringe as a first instinct when I see a notice of a review of one of my books. Most of the time, reviews are relatively neutral ("this book had these strengths and these weaknesses"). Once in a while, they are good ("this was an incredibly insightful work!"). But sometimes, reviews are bad ("this book did not meet expectations") and occasionally ugly ("this book stinks"). One of the earliest reviews of my dissertation monograph was not positive. I was devastated. Here I was, a new academic, having put my blood, sweat, and tears into my first major publication, and the first guild reaction was not what I wanted. I was discouraged and a little ashamed. So, how do you handle negative reviews and academic rejection?

I've had my fair share of this, in print reviews, blog reviews, and on social media. And I have learned a lot about what *not* to do. The first thing I want to say to anyone out there who is wrestling with negative reviews is: you are not alone. It is part of the gig. To be a writer is to have people not like your writing. You will have fans and advocates, but you will inevitably have critics. The most respected and charming academics have books that are disliked by *some*one. When you read a negative review in the privacy of your home or office, it is normal to feel embarrassed and alone. But it might help to just think and know that this is a kind of true initiation into the guild.

Several years back, I was frustrated with a string of rejections from jobs that I interviewed for. I vented to some of my mentors, and then they shared all the job rejections they experienced over the years. It was surprisingly cathartic. It's not just that misery loves company. It's also about overcoming imposter syndrome. If we know that *everyone* experiences bad reviews and rejection every now and again, it normalizes the experience.

So, the first bit of advice I can give is, know that bad reviews will come and that you are not alone. Second, don't assume the worst. I am the kind of person that too often lets fears and "what ifs" take over. *What if everyone read this review? What if it ruins my reputation? My career?* It's a big world out there, trust me, everyone did not read that review about your academic book. Take a deep breath, don't turn this into an international crisis. Think about the review that's in front of you, not the potential "fallout" that you think is going to ruin your life.

Third, don't fixate on the negatives. Is the review fair and balanced? Does the author mention any positives or strengths? My tendency is to focus on the dislikes of the reviewer, but maybe in the end the review is more even-handed and I just didn't care to notice.

Fourth, be willing to learn from the review. My approach to book reviews is that they exist to contribute to an ongoing conversation. I used to think that the point of a book review was to assess whether the book was "right" or "wrong." In most cases, though, it is not that simple and easy. And maybe the reviewer is not really in the best position to make that kind of assessment. And why is that kind of assessment necessary at all? Nowadays, I prefer to see my role as a reviewer as engaging meaningfully in the book's context, ideas, and arguments (which inevitably involves some measure of critique and praise). When that happens, much can be learned from both the book and the review. So, as an author reading a review of my work, I want to be able to ask myself, *is there something I can learn from this review*? The answer to that question might be a correction, or it might be a new perspective I haven't thought about before. And, every once in a while, I genuinely think the review was off-base and I try to forget about it.

The fifth thing I want to say is this: don't respond to "murmur criticism" on social media. Murmur criticism happens when a group of readers (maybe they didn't even read it!) start to bad-mouth a book or article and the conversation snowballs into rants. Social media can be this unpredictable, mercurial, mess of immediate reactions. That can sometimes make it an unhelpful place to have deep, respectful conversations about important academic topics. If you feel that there are things "going around" about your work that are legitimately unfair and damaging, you might want to take some time to see whether it is a real problem worth addressing or not. There can be a place for a thoughtful response (on a blog, website, or magazine). But in many cases, the wisest thing is to just let it go. The sayings are true, the news cycle doesn't last forever and, to be honest, a bit of murmur criticism isn't going to kill a good academic book. Shake it off, and refocus on doing good academic work driven by the vocation or reasons that inspired you in the first place.

New Editions?

Under what circumstances does a book deserve a second (or "new") edition? If you are reading this book, chances are you are not really in an immediate position to be thinking about this, but it is a good question to ponder for down the road. Most books don't get a new edition. A new edition is an attempt by the author and publisher to prolong availability and engagement with an important work. One aspect is whether or not the book is out of print. Are people able to buy copies? If there is demand for the book, this will inspire the publisher to consider another printing. Beyond just producing more copies of the same book, one has to consider: does the content and discussion need updating? And then, how extensive should the changes be? Some writers make major changes, some just update footnotes and add a bit of nuancing here and there. And some do little to nothing with the actual main text and simply add a special reflection or "afterword."

In terms of timing, I would say generally speaking that it would take ten to twenty years for a book to gain enough traction and impact to consider a new edition. Now, textbooks *might* see a shorter timeline, because of the type and frequency of usage. Students and professors may catch mistakes or missing information that need addressing more immediately. In areas like language textbooks, there may be an advancement in scholarship that requires changes as well.

Sometimes, the publisher will approach the author and invite them to write a new edition. (The publisher might be tracking ongoing sales and notice both consistent sales over a decade, but also a recent drop that opens up an opportunity.) But the author might approach the publisher with the idea as well. Many publishers will be open to these proposals, but they will want to identify whether or not the original book has had a good enough track record of sales and a recognized impact on the field. And the new edition would need to offer something special to stimulate fresh interest.

Shaping a Writing Career

I won't pretend to have the right advice to tell you how to plan your writing career. Some writers will write a lot, others will write a little. Some will write on the same subject for decades, others will explore many different subjects. There is no one-size-fits-all way to plan your publication future. So, we won't dwell here on specifics, but rather offer some tips that have helped me think through the *what*, the *when*, and the *why* of a writing career.

Passion. Your writing, in most cases, should be inspired by your passions, those subjects that are meaningful to you. That might seem obvious, but sometimes we (writers) get asked to write things, and maybe we don't have much of an interest in the subject. That does not automatically mean that you say "no" to every opportunity that comes your way. But it does mean that you have to think through whether an invited opportunity will (a) sustain your energy and attention enough to follow through well and (b) consume your time in such a way that you *won't* be able to say "yes" to another opportunity that you care more about.

Need. I have had lots of good book or essay ideas that have never seen the light of day, because someone else published it first and better. Obviously, one factor to consider when writing and publishing is whether the work is actually necessary. Don't be that person that writes on all of the trendy topics just to be in the conversation. Hopefully, if your editor and publisher are really sharp, they will be able to help you decide if there really is a market for your book idea. The best books come to be as a result of the combination of passion, expertise, market need, and timing. Some of that is in your control, some of it isn't. Focus on the elements in your control.

Opportunity. More than half of what I have written thus far in my career started with an editor asking me to write for a series or multi-contributor planned project. And obviously I said "yes." As my career has progressed, I have said "no" a lot more to these invitations, mostly because I want to focus on my own "passion projects." Those invited opportunities were helpful in my early career for making new friendships, learning the ropes of publishing, and exploring new topics. I don't regret those opportunities, just because I can't accept them now as often.

Collaboration. A key factor in which projects I say "yes" to is the "who"— who asked and who's involved? Sometimes, I get excited about working with particular scholars more than the topic itself. It is also about forming strategic relationships and partnerships with a view towards the future. Sometimes, I have reached out to people I want to edit and write with. Other times, they have reached out to me. One of the assumptions behind this happening is that you are engaged with "guild life" enough that you are rubbing shoulders with other scholars and making friendships and connections. Many opportunities start with an unplanned hallway conversation at a conference.

Time. Several years back, a very senior-level scholar was asked to write a major commentary. He turned down the very prestigious offer. I asked him why. He said that, though the possibility was attractive and worth considering, he didn't want to have that massive commitment hanging over his head for what could be a decade or more of his career. I thought that was a wise decision to consider how much space he had in his research schedule in the long term. You can only do so much. So, opportunities need to be weighed carefully.

Balancing Multiple Projects at Once

While some writers like to work on projects one at a time, this is not always possible, especially when we take into consideration invited projects with firm deadlines. So, inevitably you find yourself juggling two or three things at once. Is there a secret to balancing projects? A key thing for me is having deadlines clear in my personal calendar. These are easy things to lose track of, so you might want to set reminders for yourself in advance (like a calendar reminder a week or two before deadlines).

Each individual project might have its own unique style guide for citation. If you are working on several things at once, it is easy to get those confused. Sometimes, I will write a short set of citation examples into my notes for each project, so I can use that as a quick reference. Of course, if you use bibliography management software, you can set those to use the preferred style for each project.

If you are running behind on multiple projects at once, which ones do you prioritize? There are a lot of factors involved in answering that question, but all things being equal, I tend to focus on anything that involves multiple contributors (e.g., an edited volume), because I wouldn't want *my* essay to hold up the whole project. If there are all solo-author projects, I would start with the nearest deadline. Be in communication with your editors and update them on delays and new projected submission dates. As we have been emphasizing all along, writing is a team activity, a partnership between author and publisher. So, clear and timely communication is crucial to maintaining good relationships.

The Writer

This chapter has focused on work that is done *after* a book is published. The writer plays a role in supporting the life of the book. Too often, academic authors in particular change gears and immediately begin working on the next project. But a little bit of work of getting the book some attention and connecting it to the right communities can go a long way towards meeting the wider goal of making an impact. In the end, "The Writer" is not just a writer. They are trying to influence, impact, change, transform, engage, provoke. The book is a means to that end. And so it makes sense the writer does everything they can to get that message out.

APPENDIX A

A Narrative Personal Bibliography

I THOUGHT IT MIGHT be helpful for some readers if I offer my own experience in writing and publishing over the last ten to fifteen years. This is not a blueprint for anyone else, but a personal reflection on my own journey, especially what I have learned about my preferences. Readers might want to know how I came to write the things I have published, which opportunities were invited (or not), and what I have learned along the way.

Phase One: Understanding the Academy (2008–11)

Traditionally speaking, an academic writer's career formally begins with the dissertation. I studied for my PhD at the University of Durham under the dual supervision of Dr. Stephen C. Barton and Professor John M. G. Barclay. My topic was Paul's non-atonement cultic metaphors in the undisputed letters. Using conceptual metaphor theory, I was interested in how his cultic metaphors served the purposes of shaping his churches' community identity and ethos. My dissertation passed in 2009.

I had heard that it was best to seek publication as soon as possible. All things being equal I think this is wise. For one thing, it really doesn't get easier to find time to revise and publish later for most people. Also, the oral defense feedback was fresh in my mind. Of course, publication shouldn't happen hastily. I was eager to be done with the dissertation. But I wanted to get it out there into the wider scholarly world, and with that in mind I wanted to find a proper monograph series. Now, I have seen recently-passed scholars try to publish their dissertation as a "regular book"—that

Appendix A

is, an academic book transitioned towards a wider audience. There may be cases where this is appropriate and helpful, but my own work fits into the majority of dissertations that would only serve a small group of researchers. I had a few New Testament monograph series in mind. Many of my peers were publishing with Mohr Siebeck (WUNT series) or T. & T. Clark's Library of New Testament Studies (LNTS). These are both reputable series. In my mind, the top series was that of the Society of New Testament Studies with Cambridge University Press (SNTSMS). I think I was too intimidated to send it there, honestly. I didn't want to wait several months for peer review, only to get rejected.

During my doctoral research, I had occasionally come across volumes in de Gruyter's Beihefte zur Zeitschrift für die neutestamentliche Wissenschaft series. I knew that James D. G. Dunn, emeritus Lightfoot Professor of Divinity at Durham, was on the series board. He was a mentor and friend. Also, I thought that it would be prestigious to publish with a European press, in this case German-based, and to be honest I really liked the production quality of the books. So, I sent it to them about six months after completing my viva (after making some changes and additions recommended by my examiners). An editor at de Gruyter got back to me pretty quickly (a few months) with a note of acceptance. They did not require any major revisions, only correction of typos. My monograph appeared in 2010: *Worship That Makes Sense to Paul: A New Approach to the Theology of Paul's Cultic Metaphors*.

Now, during my PhD study, I also published a few academic articles. Firstly, I wanted the experience of article publishing; perhaps more importantly, I knew that when it came to job hunting, an article or two on the CV would perhaps catch the eye of search committees sifting through many dozens of applications. I had a priority list of journals that I wanted to publish with. My first major academic publication was with *Journal for the Study of the New Testament*.[1] I had been doing research on 1–2 Thessalonians for my dissertation, and in the course of doing some translation work, I had some thoughts on the use of the Old Testament in 2 Thessalonians. I wrote the article and sent it off to *JSNT*. I had no idea how the process worked, whether my article would get accepted or heavily criticized. To my surprise, it was accepted on the condition of "major revisions."

Looking back now, I did a pretty bad job revising it (again, I didn't know what I was doing). The editor at the time worked with me to get the

---

1. Gupta, "Apocalyptic Reading of Psalm 78," 179–94.

article into good shape for final publication. I remember feeling a strange mixture of self-disappointment at the need for such major and ongoing revisions, and also encouragement at the prospect of publishing with a major journal. This uncomfortable feeling of discouragement and pride has continued throughout my career (now almost fifteen years later). The academic life is one of continual rejection and criticism, and at the same time occasional acceptance. I don't know very many colleagues who experience mainly "highs" or "lows." I suppose there is a strange comfort and challenge in this: there is little time to celebrate victories before the next notification arrives; and likewise if you are wallowing in "yet another rejection," just keep refreshing your email. Good news will come.

Towards the end of my doctoral studies, and in the period just after, I published a few articles related to my dissertation topic. Two of these articles came from material that was cut from the dissertation. I reshaped them into independent arguments and discussions and sent them off.[2] Journals were chosen according to the periodical "fit." For one of these, it was rejected by my first choice, so I made the natural choice of seeking out another option. Another two articles engaged with my dissertation subject, but with interest in method and wider conversations in the biblical studies academy.[3]

In this early phase in my career, I was blessed with the opportunity to co-write an article with a more experienced colleague, Fred Long (Asbury Seminary). Fred and I were just acquaintances at the time, but he knew through social media of my interest in Ephesians and empire. He was, at that time, writing on the same subject, so he reached out to me with the idea of co-authoring an article. So we did.[4] It was a lot of fun. I had never collaborated in writing with another scholar before. I wrote the "bones" of the article, sketching out the big ideas and major transition points. Fred was able to fill in loads of details, academic scholarship, and he smoothed out the prose. Then we went back and forth a few times with adjustments until we were both satisfied with the final product. We sent it to a journal and it was accepted. Since then, I have co-written and co-edited many projects—I think this unexpected initial experience, a very positive one, warmed me over to collaboration.

---

2. Gupta, "Royal Priesthood, Honored and Chosen"; Gupta, "Cultic Metaphors in Philo."

3. Gupta, "Towards a Set of Principles"; Gupta, "Whose Body Is a Temple?"

4. Gupta, "Politics of Ephesians and the Empire?"

Appendix A

The last publication I will mention in this phase of my career is my book, *Prepare, Succeed, Advance: A Guidebook for Getting a PhD in Biblical Studies and Beyond* (2011). The book actually began as a series of blog posts that I wrote in 2007–8.[5] To be honest, when I was preparing to do a PhD, I didn't really know what I was doing. I was learning a lot about academic life as I had new experiences like responding to a "Call for Papers," or writing a book review. Now, there was already advice about academia online on websites and blogs, but very little on biblical studies in particular. So I sought to fill that gap, to demystify the early academic journey.

The response to my blog posts was overwhelmingly positive amongst grad students considering doctoral work. But when I decided that I wanted to write a book-length treatment of the subject, by and large publishers and established scholars thought it was not a good idea. This kind of information, they said, is not meant to be published in a book; it was the kind of thing shared in conversation and mentorship. I understood that, and it definitely made me reconsider whether or not it was worthwhile. I was just a newly minted scholar, fresh out of a doctoral program, but I pressed on because I knew there were so many students out there—like me—who were often uncomfortable asking for help and advice. And I knew some students didn't have mentors ready and willing to give them academic advice. Indeed, I have found women and scholars of color especially didn't have the personal mentorship networks to "get a leg up" in the academy. "How-to" books serve them by giving access to helpful information equally available to all, and not just to the special "somebodies" who have readily available mentors and academic networks.

The first few publishers I approached were polite, but clearly not interested. The audience was too small (PhD hopefuls in biblical studies), I was a green and unknown author, and I was giving subjective advice. Though I was feeling discouraged, I wasn't quite ready to give up. I remember having a conversation with an early career editor at Wipf & Stock, Dr. Chris Spinks, at the annual SBL conference and I shared my book idea with him, bracing myself for yet another "Sorry, I don't think this project is right for us" response. To my surprise, Chris thought it was a project worth pursuing, and the rest, as they say, is history. For almost a decade of my early career, that book has been one of the most widely read and reviewed books I have produced. In 2019, Wipf & Stock enthusiastically published a second edition with expanded and updated material.

5. See https://www.patheos.com/blogs/cruxsola.

A Narrative Personal Bibliography

That wraps up "Phase One" of my writing career, that period when I was getting my footing in the world of writing. I look back with some embarrassment when I think about some sloppy writing, my thin skin when it came to receiving critical feedback, and a few articles I wrote that were rejected numerous times and never saw the light of day. But finishing a PhD is a major accomplishment and I look back with appreciation for surviving that experience. I also learned how a manuscript becomes a book, how to publish smaller projects like academic articles, and the joy of co-writing with a friend.

I should mention that I wrote and published many of these things while helping to take care of my family (my kids were born in 2006, 2009, and 2011). My wife did much of the child care while I was studying and then later working at various institutions. We lived in three different places between 2008–11 (Durham, England; Ashland, Ohio; Seattle, Washington). It is unfair to imagine that most early career scholars have the luxury of sitting peacefully in repose in one's office, writing on a laptop while sipping whiskey with Yo-Yo Ma playing in the background. After I finished my PhD, writing often happened in the dark hours of the early morning or late at night; reading and research occurred in little snippets when time could be stolen during a baby's nap or while the kids were on a playdate. Forget whiskey and cello music, heck, forget the office! Until I was settled into my career (about seven years after my PhD), I didn't do most of my writing in an office. (For some of those years, I didn't even *have* an office.) I wrote in bed, on the couch, or in the car sitting in a parking lot. *When do academics write, you ask?* Anytime they can find time. *Where do they write?* Anywhere they can plug in their laptop. Everyone has different research and writing habits, but the point I want to make here is this: please don't imagine that others have this perfect life where they sit in a fully-stocked library all day on Tuesdays and Thursdays, and write in their large, luxury office Monday and Wednesday, and then go golfing all day Friday. I don't know anyone who enjoys that lifestyle. I assume the vast majority of academics, especially early career professors, carve out research time whenever they can, and chip away at their writing projects bit by bit until they can get the thing done.

Appendix A

Phase Two: Participating in the Academy (2011–18)

If the first phase of my writing career was about learning the basics of research and publication, my second career era was about developing a long term research agenda and contributing to the field of New Testament studies in broader ways, beyond my dissertation topic. Everyone shapes their writing career in their own unique way; there is no one-size-fits-all. I don't pretend to be a model for others. Some people write a lot. Some write less. Some write lots of short pieces, like academic articles. Others prefer the long monograph. Others still excel at editing and bring together various experts and voices. There comes a point where it becomes clear what your writing strengths are and where you are best positioned (by personality, passion, and education) to serve the academy and reading public. It became apparent to me that I have found a niche in the area of reference resources, especially commentaries.

After publishing my dissertation monograph and my book on doctoral studies, I really did not have a clear sense of a topic I wanted to explore in another book. Thankfully, my next project came by invitation. The invitation came through an important friend and mentor, Dr. Todd Still. Back in 2007, I was presenting my research on Philippians at the British New Testament Society conference in Exeter (UK). Todd, though living in the USA, made the trip across the pond to attend the conference, and he happened to be present at my paper. It was my first academic conference presentation ever. I was so nervous, because many of my academic heroes were sitting in the audience staring at me: Morna Hooker, Howard Marshall, Bruce Longenecker, and Todd (another former student of John Barclay, from his days at Glasgow). Todd kindly chatted with me about Philippians scholarship (he was working on a Philippians commentary at the time). That sparked a friendship that has grown over the years. Fast forward a few years later, and Todd told me that there was an opening in the commentary series he was publishing in (Smyth & Helwys Bible Commentary). The original contracted writer for Colossians could not write that volume, and Todd wanted to bring my name to the editors. Thanks to his support, they were persuaded to ask me. I am one of those weird people that loves to read and collect commentaries. I own many dozens of them, I like how they look, I like the format, I use them a lot in research—and I was thrilled to have a chance to write one.

Thankfully, by the time I started to write my volume on Colossians, many volumes in the series were published, so I had plenty of examples to follow. I had to learn a method of researching and writing a commentary (there is no instruction booklet for the process!), but I did devise a basic approach that has served me well now several commentary projects later. As I did with my dissertation, I wanted to utilize my commentary research to produce some smaller projects as well. So I wrote two articles on Colossians. This is one of the little "secrets" to my productivity. Find ways to use your research more than once (but not word-for-word). You don't want to keep repeating yourself, of course, but if you start out a project thinking you might get a few articles out of it as well, then it stays in your mind to see how a smaller piece of the bigger whole might find its way into a journal, a magazine article, or a short essay.[6]

In this phase of my career, I was also writing a lot of course lectures. After my PhD, I bounced around from job to job, because permanent jobs were just not available. I spent time at Ashland Theological Seminary (2009–10), Seattle Pacific University and Seminary (2010–12), Eastern University (2012–13), Northeastern Seminary (2013–14), and Portland Seminary (2014–19). Most of these positions were not tenure-track, so I knew my time there was limited. As I went from place to place, I received a new slate of courses and I had to produce new lecture material. Occasionally some lecture notes became material for publication. I remember teaching the Gospel of John a few times. In the course of my study of John, I discovered some interesting connections between John and Sirach. While I do not consider myself a Johannine scholar, I was excited to publish on John.[7]

This era of my career was also marked by trying new things. One such endeavor was publishing a Festschrift honoring two of my friends and mentors at Durham, Stephen Barton and Bill Telford.[8] Both of them retired from their positions around the same time, ending very fruitful careers. They were both extraordinarily humble scholars and mentors, and I felt that their scholarship ought to be celebrated. So, I thought, what if we could celebrate them both together in one Festschrift? After all, they taught at the same institution, they were good friends, and they both published on the Synoptic Gospels (among other things). First, I enlisted the co-editorial help of my friend and fellow Durham grad, Kristian Bendoraitis. Then, together we approached T. & T. Clark. They were enthusiastically supportive of a

6. Gupta, "What Is in a Name?"; Gupta, "Beholding the Word of Christ."
7. Gupta, "Gloria in Profundis."
8. Bendoraitis and Gupta, *Matthew and Mark across Perspectives.*

Appendix A

volume honoring these two gentlemen. From there, Kristian and I crafted a basic proposal—we would focus on Matthew and Mark and a diversity of methods that illuminate academic study. Then we reached out to potential contributors, especially friends and students of the honorees. A majority of the people we invited said yes, and it shaped up to be a wonderfully rich collection of essays.

Around the same time we were getting the Festschrift project started, I got an email from Mike Bird, inviting me to write for the New Covenant Commentary Series that he co-edited with Craig Keener. As with the case with the Smyth & Helwys series, someone else had backed out of a contract, in this case for 1–2 Thessalonians. Mike knew of my work on Colossians and asked me to write on Paul again. In general, I approached this commentary the same as I did for Colossians. But I would say the major difference is that I was learning how to find my own authorial voice. With the Colossians commentary, I was so worried about being wrong that I was perhaps overly cautious not to step outside of conventional views. With 1–2 Thessalonians, I pushed myself to advocate for my own fresh readings and thoughts.

In 2017, I began to take more initiative in pursuing fresh scholarship opportunities; in this case, it was designing an intermediate Greek textbook, and enlisting a group of seminary students to help me write it. I applied for a grant to fund a special e-textbook project through my institution at the time, George Fox University/Portland Seminary.[9] My students were learning advanced Greek, and what better way to learn than by learning how to teach the subject? Each week, the students in the course would work on the same Google document, writing in different colors, so I could see who was doing what. They were studying the Greek text of Galatians (and related texts from the Septuagint and early Christian literature), and as they learned about syntax, grammar, and semantics, they created "study notes" that went into the book. The next week, they would double-check each other's work and refine the notes. We did this for about thirty weeks, and by the end we had an excellent textbook created by the students. The best part—my seminary students learned the power of giving something free to the world. Their hard work was not just for a grade, and not even just for a good learning experience, which they certainly gained. They got a chance to turn their energy into a book that has been downloaded over five

---

9. See "Intermediate Biblical Greek Reader: Galatians and Related Texts" at https://digitalcommons.georgefox.edu/pennington_epress/2/.

thousand times all over the world with major download sites in the USA, UK, Brazil, Canada, Australia, Indonesia, South Korea, the Philippines, Egypt, and India.

The last major project that came out of this phase of my life was yet another commentary, but a unique one. Through my work with Smyth & Helwys, I got to know the president of the press as well as the series editors. They invited me to participate in a supplement series, niche commentaries that explore a key text or theme from Scripture. I had such a good experience with Smyth & Helwys with my Colossians commentary, I was eager to work with them again. It didn't take long for me to decide on the topic, I wanted to write on the Lord's Prayer. Again, in this project I felt more free to "be myself" in my writing, to be more prescriptive, to disagree with conventional scholarship, and to explore new angles and approaches to the various interpretive conundrums of academic scholarship on the Lord's Prayer.

Phase Three: *Contributing to the Academy* (2018–22)

In 2019 and 2020, I published a handful of books in a short period of time. As experienced writers know, the books might come out within a few months of each other, but that doesn't tell the tale of their writing history. For example, I wrote one book (*The New Testament Commentary Guide*) in a matter of a few months. It was a light and fun project, it didn't require loads of academic research, and it was produced relatively quickly by Lexham Press. Another book, my Zondervan Critical Introduction to 1–2 Thessalonians, began in 2013 (when I was invited) and I worked on it steadily until late 2018, published in 2019. Let's briefly go back to 2013. I was working on my New Covenant Commentary on 1–2 Thessalonians for series co-editor Mike Bird. Not long after Mike invited me for that project, as editor for the Zondervan Critical Introductions he asked me to do 1–2 Thessalonians in that series as well. It made sense to me: I could do the heavy research required for the Zondervan Critical Introduction, and apply that to the much shorter commentary in the New Covenant Commentary Series.

Not long after I accepted the Zondervan project in 2013, I began to have conversations with Baker Academic about a textbook idea. Baker had published a handy theology volume called *Across the Spectrum: Understanding Issues in Evangelical Theology* (Gregory Boyd and Paul R. Eddy), which

Appendix A

surveyed the major views on several debated theological issues throughout history and today. I thought it would be helpful to have a similar volume on New Testament studies. That eventually became the book *A Beginner's Guide to New Testament Studies*.

A few years later, Scot McKnight reached out to me and asked me if I would write the Galatians volume for the Story of God Bible Commentary series (Zondervan Academic). To be honest, I was eager to work with Scot and I really enjoyed how the series was developing. Also, I had taught Galatians a few times and looked forward to diving deeper into Galatians scholarship.

By 2016, I had developed a bit of a friendship with Scot, so I boldly approached him with the idea of producing a second edition of *The Face of New Testament Studies*. I had noticed that the first edition was about fifteen years old, and clearly could benefit from an update with new authors and chapters. Scot had originally co-edited *The Face of New Testament Studies* with Grant Osborne. Grant was not able to work on a second edition, so Scot and I ended up editing it together. Over many emails and text messages we chose the key topics we wanted to address and the contributors we wanted to invite. About a year later, IVP Academic invited me to serve as an associate editor for the second edition of the *Dictionary of Paul and His Letters*, with Scot serving as the general editor and Lynn Cohick as another associate editor.

While I had these exciting writing projects going on, I felt that it was also time that I wrote another monograph. It had been several years since I published my dissertation. Yes, I enjoyed writing commentaries and textbooks, but the stand-alone book has a unique power to generate discipline-shaping conversation. I decided to write on Paul's faith language. I had explored Paul's use of *pistis* language in my work on Colossians, 1–2 Thessalonians, and Galatians. I had begun to work on a commentary on Philippians as well (co-written with Mike Bird, for the New Cambridge Bible Commentary). In that wide-ranging commentary work, I felt that, aside from the often mundane *pistis Christou* debate, Pauline scholarship generally neglected Paul's faith language. I had one publisher in mind for this: Eerdmans. There was a simple reason for this. One of my mentors at Durham, and a great inspiration to me as a writer, was James D.G. Dunn, and Dunn had a close publishing relationship with Eerdmans. He published his massive *Theology of Paul the Apostle* with Eerdmans, and his Christianity in the Making series, as well as several shorter works. I approached (then-Eerdmans editor) Michael Thomson with my book idea, and after some tweaks and revisions to my proposal, I signed a contract. This was my dream and it became a reality. Moreover, Dunn kindly wrote the foreword to the book, which I will always treasure.

As I complete this book, I have a few new projects I am working on. I have completed a kind of companion book to *A Beginner's to New Testament Studies*; it is called *Fifteen New Testament Words of Life*. The gist of the book involves my description of fifteen important thematic words like faith, love, life, righteousness, holiness, peace, witness, etc. I got the idea from the general work I do on New Testament commentaries. Some of these "load-bearing" words appear quite a lot in Paul's letters (where I tend to do research). I have noticed that Christians today often take the meanings of these words for granted, since we have equivalents of their Greek words in English. But what *exactly* did the NT writers mean when they used *agapē* (which we translate "love")? Or *eleutheria* ("freedom")? I walk through biblical usage (with one particular NT text per word) and then process how we might reflect on that theme today using our own common language and meaningful cultural analogies. I began writing this book a few years back, and I had an idea for how I might "field-test" the chapters. After doing some preliminary research on each of the chapters, I made a plan to collect student feedback. That year, I was teaching a New Testament introduction class on Monday evenings. So, on Monday morning I would sit at my office desk and basically write out a book chapter using some basic notes I jotted down. I would write until I got to about 3,000 words. I would add incomplete footnote references, and I would put a symbol (like ###) where I needed more technical information. The goal was to write up a very rough draft. So, I might start at ten in the morning and finish around one in the afternoon. If I didn't get a complete draft done, so be it. Then, I would print out a copy of the draft for each person in the class (~twenty people in all, if I recall). During my three-hour class on Monday evenings, I planned to dedicate about an hour to sharing with my students and receiving their feedback. I decided to read the chapter out loud. Periodically, I would stop (at the end of a section), and ask them to jot down their feedback: positive, corrective, suggestive, whatever. At about halfway through and at the end of each one-hour weekly reading of my manuscript, there would be time for group discussion and reflection. We did this for about a dozen weeks. It was a great way for me to share my research with my students, and I benefited hugely from their verbal and written feedback (I collected their scribbled feedback, if they wanted to share). I wanted to share this little story with you, because I have gravitated towards a place in my career where I want my research, writing, and editing to be more collaborative. Too often writing is a solitary and lonely experience. Private writing can be good, going on a retreat with one's own thoughts and all that. But for most of my book projects, my experience has been that the more feedback during and just after the writing (and before publication), the better.

The other major project of 2021 was completing my Galatians commentary (Story of God Bible Commentary Series, Zondervan Academic). My first major experience diving into Galatians scholarship was when I taught a seminary course on Galatians in 2013 (when I was teaching at Northeastern Seminary of Roberts Wesleyan College). Scot McKnight approached me in 2015 with an invitation to write for SOGBC. I had written a few commentaries beforehand, and I enjoyed that experience, so I agreed. I had to put this project on the back burner for a few years to clear up my writing schedule. I worked on Galatians in earnest starting in 2018. Working through the scholarship and writing the more exegetical parts of the commentary were pretty easy and comfortable. What was especially challenging was writing the "Live the Story" sections, which focus on modern application and embodiment of the teachings in each passage (think of them like little devotionals, illustrative stories, or sermons). Some of the material I came up with was good, but sometimes my series editors (Mike Bird and Scot McKnight) gently sent me back to the drawing board. I was happy to make edits and changes. Over the years, I have learned not to be embarrassed or upset when editors ask me to remove something or make a major change. They care about the project and they want the work to flourish and make a difference.

How did I end up writing this book, *The Writer*? I am asked from time to time to teach research methods. And it seems like I give the same walkthroughs and advice every time. It makes sense to have a book version of my advice that can be accessed by anyone anywhere. For many of my writing projects, I start with: *what do I wish I had as a student?* And then I try to produce something that I would have benefited from.

Reflections

Does my writing career thus far say something about me as a writer? I hope so. If I had to evaluate myself—it's been fun to look back at old emails with co-editors, publishing editors, contributors, and co-writers—I would say the following.

I like to write. For some academics, writing is a chore; it is a necessity, but it isn't life-giving. The opposite is true for me. I don't write because my job requires it. I write because I love to write. I love almost every aspect of writing from the ideas phase, to outlining, to the writing, and even proofreading and revising. (I don't like creating an index, that's the worst.) It's okay if you don't love to write. You can still write. But it's important to know yourself and to be honest with yourself. If, like me, you love to write, I would suggest making more clear plans about how you are going to channel that energy and passion. My story meanders and I probably said "yes" to too many invitations, perhaps because I got so excited about writing. Only after some trusted colleagues encouraged me to be more intentional and selective did I sit down and think: *what is my passion? What are the topics that I care a lot about?*

If you know that writing is not your passion, then you need to learn how to be disciplined and make a plan for getting the work done. Maybe it is not your favorite thing to do, but with the right support systems in place, I am sure you can find a way to make it less painful.

I love working with other people. Writing can often be a solo experience. And some people like it that way. I can see, looking back, that I love to co-edit and co-write. It's fun for me to get excited with someone else about new ideas and opportunities, and then to execute a writing project together—and eventually to celebrate together. When Kristian Bendoraitis and I got to surprise Stephen Barton and Bill Telford with their Festschrift, it was a special and memorable moment. (Barton was one of my doctoral supervisors.) For Barton, we had a dinner at SBL with him, he had no idea the Festschrift was coming, and when we pulled it out and showed it to him, I will always remember two things: (1) the surprise on his face, and (2) the big grin on Kristian's face. I had two more blessed opportunities to be a part of surprise Festschrifts (Michael Gorman and Scot McKnight). I cherish these wonderful occasions to honor my mentors and work on a love project with good friends.

I have co-written scholarship on a few occasions. It is sometimes difficult work, to smooth out the choppiness of two writing styles coming together. But for me, the joy and synergy far outweighed the challenges.

I like to explore different topics. Some writers have honed their craft and stay focused on one subject or sub-discipline. They are content to operate

Appendix A

in one area for a decade or their whole career. I am not one of those people. If you dared me to write on 2 Maccabees, I would probably do it. I am a curious person, I am a "generalist," I like to learn about different subjects, and I am *not* as interested in doing deep dives in a very narrow subject for a very long time. I don't think any of this is good or bad. We need generalists (especially helpful for writing textbooks) and we need specialists (who write those discipline-shaping, formative monographs). *Know thyself.* You don't need to be boxed in or feel guilty because you are one or the other. Enjoy what you do, play to your strengths, challenge yourself once in a while, and don't worry about what other people are doing. Look inside your own writing soul and let whatever books come out that are inside of you.

I prefer to write short books. All of my books combined don't amount to the total word count of one of Craig Keener's tomes. Now, I love Craig's books, I have most of them, I read them, I cite them, I benefit from them, he has a gift. But that's not me. Generally speaking, I aim for the 200-page slim book, not the 800-page paper tank. I don't have the attention span or energy to endure writing a massive work. That's okay. I do an exploratory treatment and then I move on.

I often write for seminary students and pastors. Most of my books are aimed at my students, ministry leaders with some theological education. I don't tend to write for the layperson, nor do I write for the "high academy." I found my audience niche.

It was harder than I thought to write this appendix, because I didn't do a good job of planning out my writing career intentionally, and I didn't do a good job of journaling about my experiences along the way. I had to look through old emails to piece together how I went from one project to another. I encourage you to chronicle your story as a writer, because it will give you opportunities to reflect on your journey.

APPENDIX B

Writing and Publishing Advice from Editors in Biblical Studies

In 2020 and 2021, I ran a blog series called "The Editors behind the Great Books in New Testament Studies."[1] I interviewed eight experienced and respected publishing editors at some of the best academic presses in the business (including Eerdmans, Baker Academic, Zondervan Academic, Wipf & Stock, Hendrickson Publishers, and Baylor University Press). The goal was to offer readers (mostly seminary students and doctoral researchers) a window into the publishing world and the expert eye of real-life acquisitions editors. I encourage you to read the blog series and take in the advice and perspective of each editor. But I thought it might be helpful in this book to consolidate their collective wisdom. Rather than quote each person individually, I will summarize their advice in broad brushstrokes. (Unsurprisingly, many of them had the same or similar advice—that's good to know!)

Making a Good Book Pitch

I asked each editor to talk about how writers succeed in grabbing the attention of editors in a book pitch and proposal.

1. Fresh ideas: offer a new angle or take. This often comes from new methods, approaches, or sometimes bringing two things into dialogue that others have not considered before.

---

1. https://www.patheos.com/blogs/cruxsola/category/editors-behind-great-books-in-nt-studies/.

2. Timeliness: a good idea is given a big boost when it hits cultural timing just right. Authors ought to have their finger on the pulse of where interest and energy lie in their field.

3. "Know Thy Publisher": it matters that authors make a specific pitch to a specific publisher. Pitches should be tailored to the publisher, cognizant of that press's backlist, interests, audience, etc.

4. Editors are colleagues, not customer service: treat editors with peer-level respect. Many editors have advanced education, some of them have PhDs. Don't talk down to editors (*You're a fool if you pass up on this book!*). Engage with them as professionals, and expect that they will do the same. Editors are not just gatekeepers for the publishing industry; they want to forge friendships and partnerships with authors. In many cases, a good relationship builds trust (both ways) and can lead to multiple projects and longevity in academic contributions.

5. Read the room: authors will get a sense for whether the editor is interested in the idea—or not. If not, don't take it personally. Publishers only have time, money, and energy to lean into a precious few projects.

6. Author enthusiasm is contagious: believe in yourself and sell your idea. Show how and why you are curious about and interested in the topic. On the other hand, if you are overly reserved, unsure, and half-hearted, that will rub off as well.

7. Meekness is a virtue: editors often see a positive sign in authors who don't think too highly of themselves, and too lowly of others. One can express confidence without trash-talking everyone else that has written on the same subject.

Editor Pet Peeves

I also asked editors: What really irks you? They were *more than happy* to tell me.

1. The dreaded "email proposal": Use a proper form. Don't "drop" the proposal material in an email that no one wants to read. (Pro tip: use the form provided by the publisher.)

2. Overkill proposals: don't give editors a whole book worth of information. Give them enough to understand the book idea and content

in context. Editors are busy—they want clear, concise, and attractive proposals.

3. Too little information: don't assume editors are completely up to date on all academic conversation. Give them enough background and context to help them see where the proposal contributes and fits.

4. Scholar, proofread! (aka, "Physician, Heal Thyself!"): It is ironic (since most academic authors teach writing) when book proposals are littered with typos. Put the extra work into making it clean and neat.

5. The impatient author: don't expect an immediate answer ("yes" or "no") after a pitch or proposal. A good editor wants to reflect and mull things over, look carefully over the written materials, and make a decision perhaps in communication with their team.

6. The stubborn author: A good author is open to editorial feedback and peer review. The goal is a great book, and revision is an essential part of improvement. Good authors are ready and willing to go the distance.

Becoming Better Writers

Editors see lots of writing from many different kinds of people. They become keenly aware of who the "excellent writers" are. What can academic writers do to become better at this craft?

1. Know your ideal reader. Authors need to really understand them, what they know or don't know, what they care about. How they think. What makes them tick. Don't assume, really understand your readers. If you can, test your ideas on students or peers.

2. Find your voice. You are no longer a student at the mercy of a dissertation committee. Own your ideas, find your voice, put yourself out there.

3. Don't emulate academic writers. Many academics are great at research, not so great at the art of winsome communication.

4. Read great literature, fiction and nonfiction. Learn from the best. Anyone can inform, but persuasion takes skill.

5. Less is more. Learn how to write concisely.

6. Tap into your best teaching techniques. Good academic writers often draw from their successful teaching approaches and exercises. Great teachers come alongside students and help engross them in a subject. They want the student to find joy, insight, and illumination.

7. Don't rush it. Academics are very busy, and there is a temptation to hurry a book along to completion and get on to the next thing. But truly *great* writing takes time, patience, cultivation, and lots of rewriting and editing.

Thinking about "Success"

I asked editors to tell me what they consider "success" when it comes to an academic book. The natural thing to do is look at sales—numbers of books sold and overall money figures. But money and popularity don't tell the whole story, and not all books are designed for high-volume sales (think about an advanced Ugaritic textbook!). So, editors offered reflections on their own definitions of success.

1. Satisfaction: One editor wrote this: *Fulfilling your calling without losing your shirt!*

2. Impact: has the book left an impression on the audience? Publishers enjoy when a book has generated "buzz." Reading communities are excited about a book and what they are learning. It has provoked conversations, even if some reactions are bad. Books should inspire conversation.

3. Longevity. A great book is more than a flash-in-the-pan event. For most books, it should inspire people to share the book with others, start a conversation, and be passed down from one recommended reading list to another.

Much of the above advice has appeared throughout our discussion in this book, but it is helpful to have it affirmed and articulated from industry professionals in editing. Learn as much as you can as early as you can in your career, but also learn from your mistakes and be gracious with yourself.

Bibliography

Adler, Mortimer J., and Charles Van Doren. *How to Read a Book: The Classic Guide to Intelligent Reading*. New York: Touchstone, 1972.

Bendoraitis, Kristian A., and Nijay K. Gupta, ed. *Matthew and Mark across Perspectives: Essays in Honour of Stephen C. Barton and William R. Telford*. London: T. & T. Clark, 2016.

Bird, Michael F., and Nijay K. Gupta. *Philippians*. New Cambridge Bible Commentary. Cambridge: Cambridge University Press, 2020.

Docherty, Susan. *The Jewish Pseudepigrapha: An Introduction to the Literature of the Second Temple Period*. Minneapolis: Fortress, 2015.

Edwards, Dennis R. "Hermeneutics and Exegesis." In *The State of New Testament Studies*, edited by Scot McKnight and Nijay K. Gupta, 63–82. Grand Rapids: Baker Academic, 2019.

Evans, Craig A. *Ancient Texts for New Testament Studies: A Guide to the Background Literature*. Grand Rapids: Baker Academic, 2012.

Freedman, David Noel, ed. *The Anchor Bible Dictionary*. 6 vols. New Haven, CT: Yale University Press, 2008.

———. *Eerdmans Dictionary of the Bible*. Grand Rapids: Eerdmans, 2019.

Gorman, Michael J. *Elements of Biblical Exegesis*. 3rd ed. Grand Rapids: Baker, 2020.

———, ed. *Scripture and Its Interpretation: A Global, Ecumenical Introduction to the Bible*. Grand Rapids: Baker Academic, 2020.

Green, Joel B., et al., eds. *Dictionary of Jesus and the Gospels*. 2nd ed. Downers Grove, IL: IVP Academic 2018.

Gupta, Nijay K. *1–2 Thessalonians*. New Covenant Commentary Series. Eugene, OR: Cascade, 2017.

———. *1–2 Thessalonians*. Zondervan Critical Introductions to the New Testament. Grand Rapids: Zondervan Academic, 2019.

———. "An Apocalyptic Reading of Psalm 78 in 2 Thessalonians 3." *Journal for the Study of the New Testament* 31 (2008) 179–94.

———. *A Beginner's Guide to New Testament Studies*. Grand Rapids: Baker Academic, 2020.

———. "Beholding the Word of Christ: A Theological Reading of Colossians." *Canadian Theological Review* 2 (2013) 21–43.

———. "Cultic Metaphors in Philo: Exploring the Question of Coherence." *Journal for the Study of the Pseudepigrapha* 20 (2011) 277–97.

Bibliography

———. *Fifteen New Testament Words of Life*. Grand Rapids: Zondervan Academic, 2022.

———. *Galatians*. Story of God Bible Commentary. Grand Rapids: Zondervan Academic, 2023.

———. "Gloria in Profundis: Comparing the Glory of Moses in Sirach to Jesus in the Fourth Gospel." *Horizons in Biblical Theology* 36 (2014) 60–78.

———. *The Lord's Prayer*. Smyth & Helwys Bible Commentary Supplement Series. Macon, GA: Helwys, 2018.

———. *The New Testament Commentary Guide*. Bellingham, WA: Lexham, 2020.

———. *Paul and the Language of Faith*. Grand Rapids: Eerdmans, 2020.

———. "The Politics of Ephesians and the Empire: Accommodation or Resistance?" *Journal of Greco-Roman Christianity and Judaism* 7 (2010) 112–36.

———. *Prepare, Succeed, Advance: A Guidebook for Getting a PhD in Biblical Studies and Beyond*. 2nd ed. Eugene, OR: Cascade, 2019.

———. "A Royal Priesthood, Honored and Chosen: Cultic Metaphors in 1 Peter." *Perspectives in Religious Studies* 36 (2009) 61–76.

———. "Towards a Set of Principles for Interpreting Metaphors in Paul." *Restoration Quarterly* 51 (2009) 169–81.

———. "What Is in a Name? The Hermeneutics of Authorship Analysis Concerning Colossians." *Currents in Biblical Research* 11 (2013) 196–217.

———. "Whose Body Is a Temple (1 Cor. 6.19)? Paul Beyond the Individualism/Communalism Divide." *Catholic Biblical Quarterly* 7 (2010) 518–36.

———. *Worship That Makes Sense to Paul: A New Approach to the Theology and Ethics of Paul's Cultic Metaphors*. Beihefte zur Zeitschrift für die neutestamentliche Wissenschaft. Berlin: de Gruyter, 2010.

Gurtner, Daniel M. *Introducing the Pseudepigrapha of Second Temple Judaism: Message, Context, and Significance*. Grand Rapids: Baker Academic, 2020.

Harder, Cherie. "Reviving Intellectual Hospitality: How to Open Our Minds, Hearts, and Homes to Our Neighbors." *Comment*, February 11, 2021. https://comment.org/reviving-intellectual-hospitality/?fbclid=IwAR0M6lUXmBs_ANWGQNJcO7JITfEAA04T7r8gdDn0aSKW79dhNgRXi3lU4qo

Keener, Craig S. *The Mind of the Spirit: Paul's Approach to Transformed Thinking*. Grand Rapids: Baker Academic, 2016.

LePeau, Andy. *Write Better: A Lifelong Editor on Craft, Art, and Spirituality*. Downers Grove, IL: InterVarsity, 2019.

Marshall, I. H., et al., ed. *New Bible Dictionary*. 3rd ed. Downers Grove, IL: InterVarsity, 2004.

McKnight, Scot, and Nijay K. Gupta, eds. *The State of New Testament Studies: A Survey of Recent Research*. Grand Rapids: Baker Academic, 2019.

McKnight, Scot, et al., eds. *Dictionary of Paul and His Letters*. 2nd ed. Downers Grove, IL: IVP Academic, 2022/2023.

Nickelsburg, George W. E. *Jewish Literature between the Bible and the Mishnah*. 2nd ed. Minneapolis: Fortress, 2011.

Olaniran, Bolane, and Indi Williams. "Social Media Effects: Hijacking Democracy and Civility in Civic Engagement." *Platforms, Protests, and the Challenge of Networked Democracy* (2020) 77–94.

Sakenfeld, Katherine Doob, ed. *The New Interpreter's Dictionary of the Bible*. 5 vols. Nashville: Abingdon, 2006–9.

Bibliography

Sparks, Kenton. *Ancient Texts for the Study of the Hebrew Bible: A Guide to the Background Literature.* Grand Rapids: Baker Academic, 2017.

Sword, Helen. *Air and Light and Time and Space: How Successful Academics Write.* Cambridge, MA: Harvard University Press, 2017.

———. *Stylish Academic Writing.* Cambridge, MA: Harvard University Press, 2012.

www.ingramcontent.com/pod-product-compliance
Lightning Source LLC
Chambersburg PA
CBHW030903170426
43193CB00009BA/730